Stronger Arms
and
Upper Body

Sean Cochran

Tom House

Human Kinetics

Library of Congress Cataloging-in-Publication Data

Cochran, Sean, 1971-
   Stronger arms and upper body / Sean Cochran, Tom House.
      p.   cm.
   ISBN 0-88011-977-2
   1. Exercise.   2. Arm exercises.   I. House, Tom, 1947-
II. Title.
GV508.C63   2000
613.7'1--dc21   99-36518
                                                                      CIP

ISBN: 0-88011-977-2

Acquisitions Editor: Martin Barnard; **Developmental Editor**: Anne M. Heiles; **Assistant Editor**: Amy Flaig; **Copyeditor**: Anne M. Heiles; **Proofreader**: Erin Cler; **Graphic Designer**: Nancy Rasmus; **Graphic Artist**: Sandra Meier; **Photo Editor**: Clark Brooks; **Cover Designer**: Jack W. Davis; **Photographer (cover)**: Peter Brouillet; **Photographer (interior)**: Tom Roberts; **Line Drawing Illustrator**: Keith Blomberg; **Mac Illustrator**: Tom Roberts; **Medical Illustrators**: Kristin Mount, except where otherwise noted. Figure 1.1 by Kathryn Galasyn-Wright, figure 1.2 by Beth Young; **Printer**: Versa

Human Kinetics books are available at special discounts for bulk purchase. Special editions or book excerpts can also be created to specification. For details, contact the Special Sales Manager at Human Kinetics.

Printed in the United States of America

10   9   8   7   6   5   4   3   2   1

Human Kinetics
Web site: http://www.humankinetics.com/

United States: Human Kinetics, P.O. Box 5076, Champaign, IL 61825-5076
1-800-747-4457
e-mail: humank@hkusa.com

Canada: Human Kinetics, 475 Devonshire Road Unit 100, Windsor, ON N8Y 2L5
1-800-465-7301 (in Canada only)
e-mail: humank@hkcanada.com

Europe: Human Kinetics, P.O. Box IW14, Leeds LS16 6TR, United Kingdom
+44 (0)113-278 1708
e-mail: humank@hkeurope.com

Australia: Human Kinetics, 57A Price Avenue, Lower Mitcham, South Australia 5062
(08) 82771555
e-mail: humank@hkaustralia.com

New Zealand: Human Kinetics, P.O. Box 105-231, Auckland Central
09-523-3462
e-mail: humank@hknewz.com

To every conditioning coach, athletic trainer,
physical therapist, exercise physiologist,
and/or fitness enthusiast out there
we have crossed paths with.
Even when we disagree,
it's better than doing nothing!

CONTENTS

ACKNOWLEDGMENTS

Thanks to the R & D employees and interns
at BioKinetics, Inc. and Functional Fitness, Inc.
Your hard work helped Sean and me to write
a better *Stronger Arms and Upper Body* book.

—Tom House

INTRODUCTION

Today's fitness enthusiasts, generally speaking, fall into three categories: those who want to *lose* what they have, those who want to *maintain* what they have, and those who want to *improve* what they have. What are your goals for a better body?

Do you want to be big and bulging, lean and sinewy, flexible and functional? How about just pain free? As you physically move through your daily activities, do you need greater muscular strength or muscular endurance? Do you want to do more with weight training or weight management? Do you need stronger arms for better swings in baseball, tennis, or golf?

Will bar curls and bigger biceps help you hit a ball harder, farther, or faster? If you are building bigger pectorals, for ball gown or swimming suit, will push-ups or bench presses be better? What does muscle stiffness or joint soreness mean? How should age or activity affect training choices for preparing or repairing your body? And how do you avoid such problems as tennis elbow or carpal tunnel syndrome?

Assume now that you have identified precisely what you want to strengthen for your upper body. Where do you get the best information and instruction on how to do it right? Should you surf the net, watch the TV sport channels, scan the sports print literature, sweat at a club, or simply let gravity rearrange your muscles?

The thought of a stronger and better upper body gets a bit muddled, doesn't it? Don't feel you're the only person confused about fitness and fatness, product and protocol. The contemporary fitness environment can be a hodge-podge of celebrity hype, misinformation, and end-user failure. In writing this book, we hope to end your frustration, however, by providing objective, up-to-date information, doable instruction—and some sustainable inspiration—to increase your chances of attaining stronger arms and a better upper body.

We aim to present clear, simple information and instruction, and help reduce your fitness dissonance while you develop your deltoids! Our mission as performance analysts has always been to *prehabilitate* people—that is, help them to live, work, and play younger and longer. We see this as a function of four performance absolutes common to both elite athletes and everyday individuals: (1) mental and emotional conditioning, (2) nutritional conditioning, (3) biomechanical movement conditioning, and (4) physical conditioning.

Together we bring to our writing task several decades of experience in professional athletics, coaching, martial arts, and bodybuilding; degrees in psychology, nutrition, biomechanics, and exercise physiology. If you review our bios, you'll see we are educated exjocks who have been through the resistance-training gamut. We work with elite and everyday athletes around the globe, applying cutting-edge sport science information with functional instruction. We try to keep our clients from making the same mistakes we first did in working toward fitness goals. We know there are no shortcuts— but also know that everybody can improve with a committed, consistent, and convenient workout program.

Stronger Arms and Upper Body is for fitness enthusiasts, bodybuilders, coaches and athletes, men and women who are looking to shape and add size, strength, or endurance (or all of these) to their chests, shoulders, and arms without compromising joint integrity or flexibility. The book is a primer for athletic coaches, personal trainers, athletic trainers, and strength and conditioning coaches who are looking to update their teaching paradigms. Every reader will find state-of-the-art information on upper body preparation specific to functional performance and the requirements of their work or play environments.

We know people's goals differ and that it's of major importance to match training protocols to specific goals. A person who's trying to lose weight, for example, will do better with total-body aerobic work and with endurance-type resistance training, because fat burning in a purely prime-mover strengthening program isn't as efficient. People who are maintaining can pick from a "smorgasbord" of old and new protocols integrated into a comprehensive series of exercises to train for range-of-motion (ROM) flexibility while building or maintaining muscle and joint integrity and function. In sequence—with integrated flexibility, bodywork, joint work, machines, and free weights— we address issues of muscle size, muscle density, muscle strength, and muscle endurance. Yes, there are some new concepts and vocabulary, with a foundation of researched and applied sport science, but you'll find the exercises are illustrated and clearly explained.

Specifics of movement come from three-dimensional motion analysis at BioKinetics, Inc. Our neuromuscular protocols for the physical preparation to support the specifics of movement come from Functional Fitness Paradigms, Inc. These Salt Lake City–based companies for years have helped athletes efficiently customize the interaction of skill work and resistance work, integrating optimal fitness with minimal risk of injury. Successes with these elite performers have paved the way for more everyday fitness pursuits. Specifically, *your* better upper body, lean or large, can be programmed and *personally* integrated. You now have the choice of aesthetics with function; you don't have to choose form over function or function over form.

Take a look at the following chart of "fictitious" profiles and protocols. It will give you an idea about the possibilities there are when planning a workout regime. It goes without saying that each one of our fictitious profiles might have any number of subprofiles.

	Body weight loss for Larry Largebelly	Body maintenance for Donna Doingfine	Bodybuilding for Bob Biggersbetter
Aerobic activity	X	X	
Integrated flexibility	X	X	
Bodywork/joint integrity	X	X	X
Machines		X	X
Free weights		X	X

Before we go further, let's take an important aside to focus on you. Obviously, as an individual you must come to terms with your "personal factors," such as motivation, time management, job, play, family, aging, and risk of injury. Exercise physiologists define training work in terms of volume, load, frequency, intensity, and duration. For you, specific training work must be defined by integrating four personal or professional performance absolutes: mental conditioning, nutritional conditioning, biomechanical conditioning, and physical conditioning. And you must consider any personal or professional constraints you may have. Please be realistic. *Your* workouts must involve *your* constraints along with whatever factors will lead to your commitment, consistency, and convenience. Unrealistic expectations lead only to frustration and failure.

Think of it this way: you are not living to work out; you are working out to enhance the quality of your life. Start by determining how much time per day and how many days per week you can consistently and conveniently commit to. Properly timed and planned, working out becomes as much a part of your day as are eating and sleeping. And, believe it or not, positive and enhancing fitness synergies carry over into every aspect of your personal and professional life. It's doable—if you do it right.

Stronger Arms and Upper Body will identify how best to integrate optimal training for both form and function. The numbers of possible workout combinations are limitless. Training at home, on the road, at the office, or in a health club are all viable alternatives. Don't worry; the book will help you with your personal inventory. And once your baseline has been established, training choices become obvious. It's excuse free if you'll let it be!

In part I we initiate a strength foundation program, discussing fitness and fitness protocols in a nontraditional approach. We give daily workouts, with total upper-body integration to involve joints; connective tissues; and large, medium, and small muscles; using single sets with multiple reps at different positions, angles, and movements. In chapters 3 and 4, we have labeled these variations and the photos that illustrate the exercise technique with corresponding numbers.

In part II we identify core exercises, giving you clear, concise directions for doing both the preparation phase and technique phase of each exercise. We update your use of both machine and free-weight exercises, suggesting how you can "periodize" workouts on different days, integrating or isolating muscle groups in single sets or multiple sets (or a combination) and working toward muscle failure. We include different position, angle, and movement protocols.

In part III we integrate the information and core exercises with functional programs. We provide a "cross-specific" approach; that is, we show sample protocols for some typical goals and profiles. We also describe how to better prepare and repair the body through active rest, stamina work, and improved blood chemistry. Finally, we help you determine if your choice of resistance-training protocols matches efficiently with your fitness profiles, making it possible to maintain or redesign continuing programs.

We had fun writing this book, and hope you enjoy reading it. More importantly, we hope it will challenge you, whatever your particular goal is, to strengthen your arms and better your entire upper body!

—Tom and Sean

PART I
STRENGTH FOUNDATION

In part I of *Stronger Arms and Upper Body* you will read about how to work the arms and upper body for function as well as form, gaining an informational base for building a strong physical foundation. Chapter 1 is about the *what* and *why* of working out. It begins with concepts and information, broadening your baseline understanding of resistance training and its importance and educating you on the anatomy of the upper body. Chapter 2 formats the *how*. Chapter 3 introduces some Pacific Rim body-training philosophy that we think facilitates the efficient interaction of the information you get in chapters 1 and 2. And chapter 4 "westernizes" the whole section, providing explanations on training the integrity of upper body joints. To accomplish this and overcome misinformation, throughout the book we'll be (1) describing positions and movements, (2) teaching you how to resistance-train with them, and (3) identifying the information that supports each protocol so you can apply it specifically to your individual work or play environment.

CHAPTER 1

Upper Body Conditioning

Training paradigms in recent years have been shifting. Five years ago we might have argued that form and function were mutually exclusive goals. Traditional philosophies of strength training and body-building, including isolation, multiple sets, large volumes, and muscle failure, didn't work for the mainstream fitness public. Most women avoided weights in dread of bulk, and men ended up quitting weights because muscle bulk didn't come fast enough or didn't replace stored fat. Even those individuals who achieved the "Schwarzenegger look" were unable to keep that look into their 30s, 40s, and 50s without injury or unreasonable commitments of time.

When it comes to using repetitive movement, in or out of the weight room, humans are only as strong as their weakest link. A strict program of heavy resistance training usually creates prime-mover strength—at the expense of synergistic strength and joint integrity between shoulder and elbow or postural stabilization within the spine and its vertebrae and discs. What we call the "bad-itises" result: bad backs, bulging discs, tendinitis, bursitis, arthritis.

On the other hand, although training for flexibility improves range of motion (ROM), it provides only marginal gains in muscle strength and endurance. So with increased job- or play-related workloads, muscle and connective tissue begins to pull and tear; structural difficulties such as stress fractures, chips, and spurs begin to show up more than they should. Muscle is the body's first line of defense with movement in work or play. However, it must be balanced—strong enough to handle external working and playing activities, but not so strong that it's out of the sequencing of internal kinetic energy. There must be a *parity* of strength, endurance, and power among the muscles, tendons and ligaments, and bones.

As you read, try to keep the following mind-set with functional strength: You're going to resistance-train specific to the positions and movements of daily activities. Legs, arms, joints, and torso are going to be stabilized before they're stressed. Starting positions and finishing positions in all resistance work will be between 90° and 180°. Hyperflexion, hyperextension, or both will be avoided in all but flexibility, or ROM, work.

Although every workout in this book is an upper body workout, the total body will be recruited whenever possible. The norm will be single sets or multiple sets or both with each exercise, and you'll use repetitions ("reps") in the position or movement within each set. Based on your personalized goals, you'll use heavy, medium, or light training days—predicated on your tolerance. You'll mix and match amounts of weight with the number of reps based on your practice, competition, job, and leisure activities. You'll avoid monotonous overtraining (neural stagnation). Weight training for bulk and brute strength, working the prime movers (the large muscle groups, or agonists and antagonists), will be balanced by working for integrity and stabilization in training the secondary movers (the small muscles, or synergists).

This approach embodies an important concept: it's possible to train for that upper body "look" and still have parity. Somewhere between big and bulky, between lean and mean, between misdirected undertraining and inappropriate overtraining, there's a workout answer for every fitness and bodybuilding enthusiast. So the good news is you can train for your ego and still do something that's healthy for your body! However, to do this—achieve levels of fitness and improve the way your body looks on the *outside*—you must also address metabolic management on the *inside* of your body.

Understanding the information and instruction that comes with this new paradigm and thinking must precede your training efforts. We've tried to simplify the concepts. Please read and reread them carefully to avoid possible confusion as you create your workout routines. If you follow the logic, it can get you around what hasn't worked before and into what will work. It can inspire you and give you the confidence to change your fitness profile.

We start with *what* training accomplishes, then explain *why* it happens—from muscle cell physiology to upper body anatomy—and, finally, tell you *how* to use baseline protocols for form and function. Our intent is to provide an up-to-date combination of the best traditional and contemporary information and instruction on resistance training.

The FIP Complex: Function, Injury Prevention, and Performance Improvement

Upper body conditioning comprises three basic areas of importance, which we like to call FIP, standing for (1) function, (2) injury prevention, and (3) performance improvement.

1. Function. The body must have a given level or capacity of strength, flexibility, and endurance to function at its optimum. The idea of function is allowing the body to move, play, or walk without any limitations. If the body does not have the required levels of muscular endurance, range of motion, strength, or flexibility, it is unable to perform biomechanical movements correctly.

2. Injury prevention. At any given time during the course of a day the body faces various specific requirements of strength, flexibility, and endurance. If your body does not have the proper levels of these factors, it becomes more vulnerable to injury. As simple a task as taking out the garbage or as complex an activity as throwing a 95-mph fastball to home plate makes demands on the body. Regardless of the task, if the body does not have the appropriate levels of strength, flexibility, and endurance, an injury occurs. And an injury resulting from such a deficit can range from a minor muscle pull to a complete tear of the rotator cuff complex in the shoulder.

3. Performance improvement. Improved performance is undoubtedly the most common idea associated with resistance training. A complete upper-body training program improves your body in all areas of importance: strength, power, flexibility, and endurance. Performance can be enhanced in a specific area or across the board, depending on your goals. An all-encompassing program will increase the strength of your entire upper body, improve your power output for performing specific movements, increase your endurance capacity, and allow for greater flexibility or range of motion in all the upper body joints.

FIP is what happens when you properly resistance-train your upper body. *Why* your body reacts to training requires an understanding of the muscles themselves. The more you know about the physiology of muscle tissue, the better your work physiology will become. Micromuscle cell physiology is all about the "little stuff" in your body. Macromuscle cell physiology is all about the "big stuff" in your body. The body itself is a system of levers (joints) and pulleys (tendons and ligaments); it's structured with bone, powered by muscle, fueled by blood chemistry, and programmed electro-chemically by the brain and nerves. Look closely at figure 1.1, the structure of muscle.

Some Basics of Muscle Physiology

Referring to images of muscle cells and the macro-/microstructure of your body, read the following definitions and explanations of muscle fibers, tissue, and actions. They can help you understand the makeup of muscles, body composition, and how the two interact during physical exertion. This basic information can also help you under-stand the physiological peaks, valleys, and plateaus—as well as the aches, pains, and stiffness—that go with preparing or repairing your body for work or play.

Macrostructure of Muscle and Muscle Fibers

Muscles in the skeletal system are divided into three levels. Each single muscle cell in the human body is surrounded by a covering of

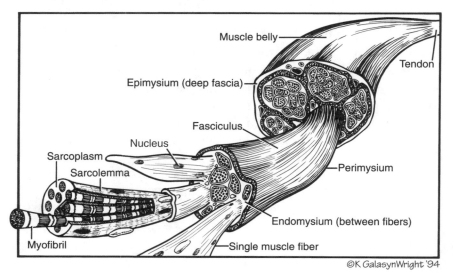

©K GalasynWright '94

Figure 1.1 The macro- and microstructure of muscle.

connective tissue known as the *endomysium*. The single muscle cells group together into bundles called *fasciculi* (sing., *fasciculus*). These bundles of muscle fiber are surrounded by a second layer of connective tissue, the *perimysium*. The final layer of connective tissue that covers all muscles in the body is known as the *epimysium*, and it not only covers all the bundles of muscle fibers but also connects them into the tendons and ligaments of the body. Tendons then connect muscle groups to the bones and joints of the skeletal system; ligaments connect bones to each other. Body movement occurs when muscle cells in muscle groups contract synergetically, pulling the tendons and ligaments, which in turn flex or extend the joints and bones.

Microstructure of Muscle and Muscle Fibers

Every muscle in the body comprises muscle fibers, nerves, and connective tissues. The muscle fiber itself consists of protein filaments, nuclei, and other chemical structures, which allow it to function. This interactive system is what we call the *microstructure*. The microstructure of the muscle consists, first, of these bundles of muscle fibers called fasciculi. Breaking them down further, we can look at a single muscle cell and its contractile properties. The muscle cells (muscle fibers) are long, and under magnification they appear striated. These cells consist of contractile proteins, a nuclei, mitochondria, myofibrils, and the sarcoplasmic reticulum. Each muscle cell contains many myofibrils, which are of great interest to us. The *myofibrils* contain the elements that allow a muscle cell to contract.

The myofibrils of a cell are composed of myofilaments. Two types of myofilaments exist in the cell: myosin and actin. And it's at this level where the contraction of entire muscle groups occurs. Each muscle cell's myofilaments move to cause contraction of the fasciculi that compose muscle in the upper body.

The theory that explains how these myofilaments, actin and myosin, function to create a contraction in the muscle cell is known as the *sliding filament theory*. This theory states that actin filaments in the muscle cell, when stimulated neurally, slide inward toward the center of the cell, or toward the myosin filaments. This movement of the actin filaments causes a contraction in the cell, and for a muscle to contract, each single muscle cell must contract simultaneously.

The central nervous system controls this contraction of muscle cells through neural impulses. A neuromuscular connection exists with each muscle in the body. Muscle fibers in the body are enervated by motor units. A *motor unit* consists of a nerve with axons that enervate a muscle cell at the neuromuscular junction to cause contraction of the cells that make up muscle tissue. This leads us to the types of muscle tissue we'll be training.

Types of Muscle Tissue

Two types of muscle cells exist in the body, categorized as Type I and Type II muscle fibers. Both types of muscle fibers contract to create muscle action, and they are physiologically similar. They differ in contraction speed, force production, endurance capability, and power output. Let's first look at Type II fibers, the fast-twitch fibers.

The Type II muscle fibers, termed fast-twitch, develop contractile force very rapidly, have a high power output, have a low aerobic capacity, and have a high anaerobic capacity. Type II muscle fibers can also be further categorized into Type IIA and Type IIB. Type IIA fast-twitch muscle fibers have characteristics of a Type I muscle fiber. That is, Type IIA fibers have a greater aerobic capacity, lower power output, and less forceful capacity than Type IIB. On the other hand, Type IIB fibers have greater force production, higher power output, but less aerobic capacity. Type II sport and fitness people are speed and quickness individuals: the sprinters, jumpers, pitchers, and hitters, for example. Type I people are more the steady, long-term "plodders": the distance runners, cyclers, and hikers.

You could say that Type I muscle fibers are almost complete opposites of Type II fibers. They have a very high aerobic capacity, more endurance, but less force and power output capabilities. Your training program can be geared toward developing either type of muscle fiber. Swimmers tend to use primarily Type I muscle fibers in their sport, for example. We discuss training strategies for each type of muscle fiber and provide you with information on putting a program together to enhance both types. But you cannot convert Type I fibers into Type II fibers. You are genetically predisposed with certain percentages of each in your genetic makeup.

Types of Muscle Action

Before delving further into the anatomy of the upper body, let's look at the different types of muscle actions the muscle fibers produce. Three types of muscle action can result from the contraction of the muscle fibers themselves: concentric, eccentric, and isometric.

Concentric Action

A concentric action in a muscle occurs when the muscle *shortens* to overcome an outside resistance. An example would be a biceps barbell curl. The biceps muscle contracts and shortens in length to resist and move the bar upward against gravity. This is a prime example of a concentric action of a muscle.

Eccentric Action

An eccentric action occurs when the muscle *lengthens* during the development of tension. Consider an example with the same biceps barbell curl. After you lift the bar upward, you extend the bar back down, in turn forcing the biceps muscles to lengthen.

Isometric Action

An isometric action occurs when the muscle produces an amount of force equal to the resistance; it therefore *maintains* its resting length. Muscle tension occurs, but the muscle neither lengthens nor shortens. An example of an isometric action would be pushing against a wall with your hands. The muscle pushing against the wall creates tension, but its length does not change.

All three of these muscle actions—concentric, eccentric, and iso-metric—are beneficial in training the upper body. Each one of them can be utilized to create greater quantities of force and power or anaerobic and aerobic qualities in your muscles. Now that we have discussed the specifics of the muscular system itself and how it functions, let's turn to the anatomy of the upper body.

Anatomy of the Upper Body and Arms

The upper body can be classified anatomically by particular body parts (see figures 1.2 and 1.3). These body parts are each composed of muscle groups. We will classify the upper body into specific segments and muscle groups, explaining the function of each group. Understand that even though we are looking at the body by separat-ing it into certain groups, the muscular systems of the body work together in integrative patterns to perform movement.

The contraction and extension of certain muscles create specific movements. The body creates these movements through the use of muscular contractions that pull the skeletal system in a range of movement patterns. In fact, our body's system of levers can *only*

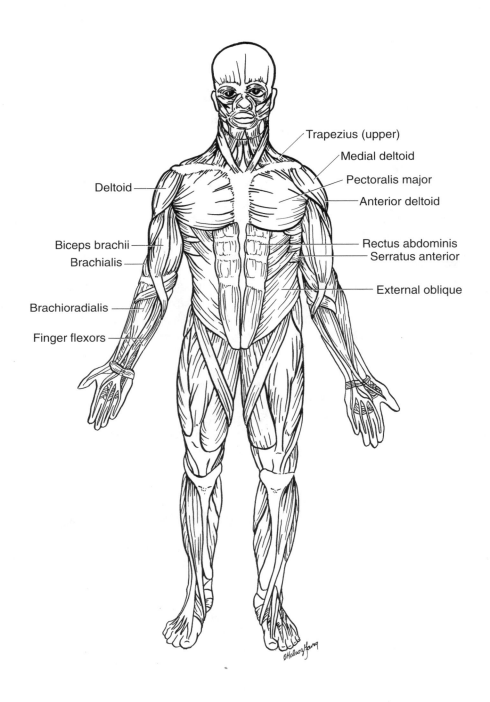

Trapezius (upper)

Medial deltoid

Pectoralis major

Anterior deltoid

Deltoid

Biceps brachii

Brachialis

Rectus abdominis

Serratus anterior

Brachioradialis

External oblique

Finger flexors

Figure 1.2   Anatomy of the male body musculature, front view.

10

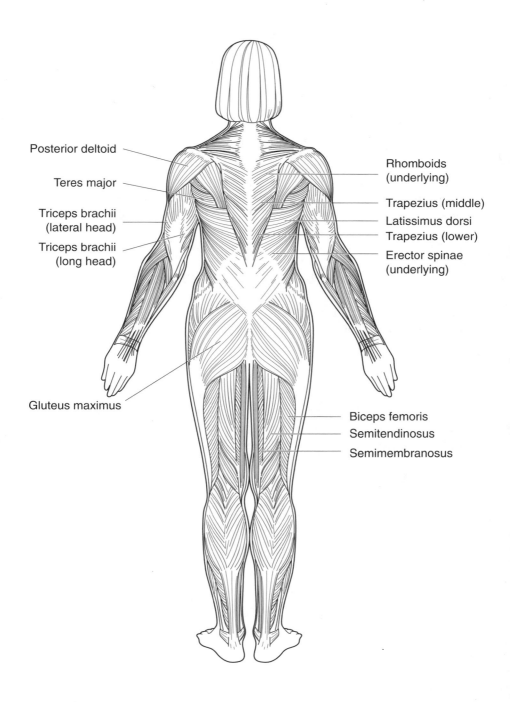

Posterior deltoid

Teres major

Triceps brachii
(lateral head)

Triceps brachii
(long head)

Gluteus maximus

Rhomboids
(underlying)

Trapezius (middle)

Latissimus dorsi

Trapezius (lower)

Erector spinae
(underlying)

Biceps femoris

Semitendinosus

Semimembranosus

Figure 1.3   Anatomy of the female body musculature, rear view.

contract or pull. However, through the use of joints and this skeletal pulley system, a pushing motion can be created. In the bench press movement, for example, weight is being pushed out from the chest. If you analyze the movement, however, in actuality the pushing is created by the joints and the contraction of specific muscles in an agonist-antagonist "pull to push."

Specific muscles (see figures 1.2 and 1.3) can be activated to perform most skeletal movements. The functioning of a muscle group coincides with skeletal movement around specific joints. The skeletal movements or actions, which are initiated by muscular contraction and extension, can be grouped into five main patterns: extension, flexion, rotation, adduction, and abduction. And the body must be resistance-trained specifically to these skeletal movements for form, function, or both.

It seems complex, right? It isn't. With a little understanding of how the skeletal and muscular systems interact, we can begin looking at specific muscle groups of the upper body. This, in turn, will lead into preparation protocols to train each group.

Chest

The main function of the chest involves contracting muscles of the shoulder joint. The pectoralis major is the predominant muscle of the chest region. The pectoral group can be separated into three sections: upper, middle, and lower. A secondary muscle in the chest is the serratus anterior, which runs along the rib cage. The serratus anterior functions to protract the scapula.

Certain exercises can be implemented to focus on a specific area of the chest. Although the chest looks relatively stable and immovable, it is the center or source of several movement patterns of the shoulder joint. There are six primary movements possible at the shoulder joint, which is freely movable:

- Abduction
- Adduction
- Extension
- Flexion
- Medial rotation
- Lateral rotation
- Circumflexion

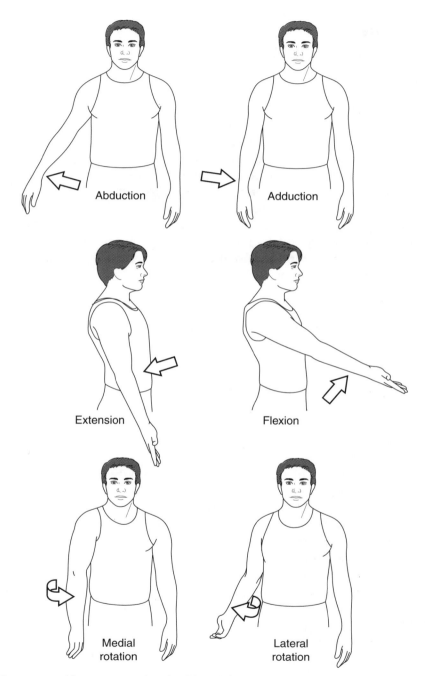

Abduction

Adduction

Extension

Flexion

Medial rotation

Lateral rotation

Figure 1.4 Movements at the shoulder: abduction, adduction, extension, flexion, medial rotation, and lateral rotation.

Shoulders

The shoulder region of the upper body consists of a single muscle named the deltoid. The deltoid, constructed in a multipennate muscular formation, works with the rotator cuff to move the upper arm in pushing, pulling, and rotating motions. These movements are able to occur due to the freely moving shoulder joint. The deltoid itself is primarily involved in abduction; flexion; and extension of the humerus, or upper arm (review figure 1.4).

The deltoid muscle can be divided into three different heads. The "heads" of the deltoid refer to its multipennate construction: a formation of the cones (heads) makes up the deltoid. The frontal head slopes over the front side of the shoulder complex. The lateral head runs down the side of the shoulder complex, and the rear head slopes down horizontally on the rear part of the shoulder. The deltoid's heads function to do different work:

- Adduction (frontal head)
- Abduction (lateral head)
- Extension (frontal head)
- Flexion (frontal head)
- Medial rotation (frontal head)
- Lateral rotation (rear head)

Biceps

The muscles of the biceps group are located on the upper part of the arms. This group consists of four muscles: the biceps brachii, brachialis, brachioradialis, and pronator teres. All four of these muscles are responsible for flexion of the elbow (see figure 1.5).

Two common terms you may encounter to describe how the biceps move are supination and pronation (see figure 1.6). *Supination* refers to the movement of externally rotating the bones (the ulna and radius) of the lower arm from the elbow joint, moving the hand toward palm-up position. *Pronation* describes the movement of internally rotating the ulna and radius from the elbow joint, moving toward palm-down position.

These are the specific functions of each of the four biceps muscles:

- Biceps brachii—flexion of the elbow joint, supination of the arm

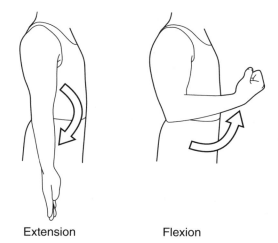

Extension   Flexion

Figure 1.5   Movements at the elbow: extension and flexion.

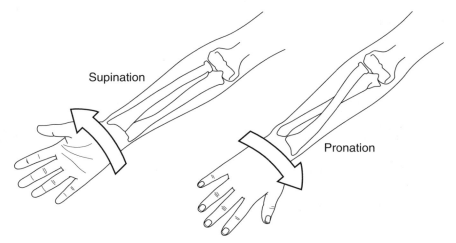

Supination

Pronation

Figure 1.6   Movements at the elbow and wrist: pronation and supination.

- Brachialis—flexion of the elbow joint; primary mover in a pro-nated position
- Brachioradialis—flexion of the elbow joint
- Pronator teres—flexion of the elbow joint, pronation of the arm

Triceps

Just as the biceps flexes the arm at the elbow, the triceps functions primarily to extend the arm at the elbow joint (see figure 1.5). The triceps, located on the back of the arm, is composed of four muscles: the triceps brachii lateral head; triceps brachii medial head; triceps brachii long head; and the anconeus. The three heads of the triceps refer to regions of the same muscle, the triceps brachii. The lateral head of the triceps is located on the lateral side of the upper arm. The long head inserts into the scapula and runs down the arm to end in the middle of the upper arm at the "common tendon." The medial head picks up where the long head ends and inserts at the elbow joint. These four muscles function together to create the following movement of extension:

- Triceps brachii lateral head—extension at the elbow joint
- Triceps brachii medial head—extension at the elbow joint
- Triceps brachii long head—extension at the elbow joint
- Anconeus—extension at the elbow joint

Rotator Cuff

The rotator cuff is located beneath the deltoid muscle in the shoulder region. The muscles making up the rotator cuff are the supraspinatus, infraspinatus, teres minor, and subscapularis. One function of the rotator cuff is support. The rotator cuff muscles actually hold the humerus (the bone in the upper arm) in place within the glenohumeral joint of the shoulder. The socket of the glenohumeral joint is very shallow, and the humerus itself would not remain in place during shoulder movements without assistance from these rotator cuff muscles and tendons. All in all, they provide stability in the shoulder joint.

The second function of the cuff muscles is to provide the rotational movements of the shoulder joint. These muscles perform three movements:

- Lateral rotation (infraspinatus, teres minor)
- Medial rotation (subscapularis)
- Abduction (supraspinatus)

Forearms

The forearm muscles function to flex and extend the wrist, hand, and fingers. The forearm muscles are separated into three layers. Each of these three layers has the function of flexing and extending the wrist, hand, and fingers. The same muscles are used for all three functions. For purposes of looking at the physiology, we can separate the muscles of the forearms into two categories: flexors and extensors. These are the flexors of the wrist, hand, and fingers:

- Flexor profundus
- Flexor pollicis longus
- Flexor superficialis
- Flexor carpi ulnaris
- Flexor radialis
- Palmaris longus

These are the extensors of the wrist, hand, and fingers:

- Extensor longus
- Extensor brevis
- Extensor indicis
- Extensor ulnaris
- Extensor digiti minimi
- Extensor digitorum
- Extensor radialis longus
- Extensor radialis brevis
- Abductor pollicis longus

Upper Back

The upper-back area comprises seven muscles having two functions. The first function is to stabilize the scapula (shoulder blade). The second function is to move the scapula. The name and function of the upper-back muscles are listed here. These muscles all function primarily to accomplish the retraction, protraction, elevation, depression, and rotation of the scapula (see figure 1.7). Each of the two scapulas is located on the posterior thorax and has no attachment to the axial skeleton. As with the stabilization function of the rotator cuff, these muscles of the upper back stabilize and move the scapula:

- Latissimus dorsi—adduction and abduction of the shoulder joint
- Trapezius—retraction, elevation, depression, and upward rotation of the scapula

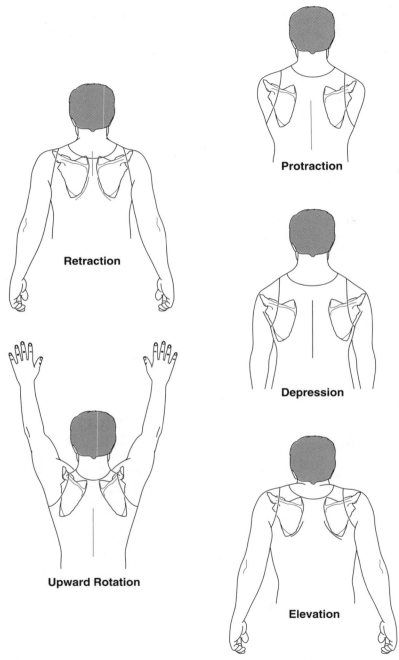

Figure 1.7 Movements at the scapulas: depression, elevation, protraction, retraction, and upward rotation.

- Rhomboid major—retraction of the scapula
- Rhomboid minor—retraction of the scapula
- Levator scapulae—elevation of the scapula
- Serratus anterior—protraction of the scapula
- Teres major—adduction, extension, and medial rotation of the shoulder joint

Torso

The final region of the upper body to outline is the torso. The torso consists of the muscles of the lower back and abdominals. We do not separate these two groups of muscles when discussing them because they function together to provide stability for the body. You can exercise them separately, but they function together. It is important to spend some good time training the torso region. Outside of aesthetics, the torso is primary to the functioning of many upper body movements in terms of *stability* and *posture* or alignment.

These are the muscles of the lower back:

- Psoas major
- Quadratus lumborum
- Spinalis group
- Erector spinae

These are the muscles of the abdominal region:

- Transverse abdominus
- Rectus abdominus
- Internal obliques
- External obliques

The abdominals and lower-back muscles stabilize, rotate, flex, and extend the trunk.

Getting to the How of Training

OK, now that we've sketched in the "who they are and what they do" of the muscles in your arms and upper body, let's add in the "how" of resistance training: How do you train for form and function? How do you train to minimize the risk of injury? How do you train to optimize performance at work or play?

Though the answers to these questions now seem simple, they didn't come easily. After 10 years of using three-dimensional motion analysis to diagnose male and female athletes competing in all sports, BioKinetics, Inc. determined at 1,000 frames per second the optimal efficiencies of body position and body movement. As a complement, the physical preparation protocols that enable individuals to achieve proper positions and efficient movements in work or play come from ongoing research at Functional Fitness Paradigms, Inc.

Humans are only as efficient as their worst positions or movements—and only as strong as their weakest links, as we have found with repetitive movement workloads in clinical and practical applications. In daily activities people absorb, direct, and deliver energy from the feet to the fingertips. Physical movement, in work or play, is the *sequential* muscle loading of kinetic-energy links.

Strength training is a specific physical movement with resistance, sequentially overloading the muscle with kinetic energy links. And with repetition, it turns out, recruiting energy *out of sequence invariably results in injury.*

Remember that muscle tissue is the body's first line of defense against repetitive movement trauma or injury. There's more. The body's second line of defense is joint and connective tissue, and its third line of defense is bone.

Do you recall our term "bad-itis"? An -*itis* is an inflammation. Tendinitis or bursitis, for example, is an indicator that your positions or movements in work or play are inefficient or your base of muscle strength and endurance isn't sufficient to support those positions and movements. The same is true with stress fractures, bone spurs, and bone chips.

Intrigued? You should be! Here's the foundation for answers to our "how-do" questions. Think of it as three-cubed (3^3). We're going to show you how to build stronger arms and an upper body for the forms and functions specific to your work or play, in 3 positions, in 3 movements, and with 3 types of resistance training (see table 1.1).

When you look at table 1.1, think of integrated flexibility as replacing traditional stretching, sort of yoga with an attitude. It's a simplification, but think of open-chain resistance as isolated movements; an example, using machines, is doing a seated leg extension. Think of closed-chain training, on the other hand, as integrated and

Table 1.1

Three positions	Three movements	Three types of resistance training
1. Straight 2. Supinated 3. Pronated	1. Linear 2. Circular 3. Angular In three movement planes: 1. Sagittal 2. Transverse 3. Frontal	1. Integrated flexibility: ROM work 2. Closed chain: bodywork 3. Open chain: *Synergists* • Light dumbbells • Elastic cord • Plyoball *Agonists* • Machine work • Free weight work

coordinated movements that involve more than one joint; examples using the body's own weight would be a squat, a lunge, push-ups, or balancing on one leg. The advantage of closed-chain exercise is that it is more like actual performance involving integrated muscular movements. Most actions are sequences of movements that involve the whole body. A squat, for example, uses the hips, knees, and ankles in sequence.

Closed-chain exercises require contact with the ground, whether with one or both hands or one or both feet. They develop prime movers but also stabilizer muscles at the joints. They can be sport-specific and are efficient. Open-chain exercises (e.g., arm curls or triceps extensions) do not require contact with the ground. They can build muscles but are less like everyday or sport motions. Synergist work and agonist/antagonist work will take place during all three types of resistance training, but they can be specifically and more efficiently integrated (in rehab and prehab) with open-chain work.

We asked in the introduction whether you seek "lean and mean" or "big and bulky." Either may be your ultimate choice for function and form. They're both OK, because they both can be done function-ally by balancing body tissue. We'll begin to look more closely at that balancing in the next chapter. You can enhance your flexibility and joint integrity by working the full range of motion. Tendons, ligaments, and small muscles (synergists) are prepared with bodywork, light dumbbells, elastic cord, and plyoball work.

You build medium and large muscles (the agonists or prime movers), on the other hand, with machine workouts and heavier free-weight work. Hypertrophic parity . . . stronger arms and upper body . . . form and function—for you, the reader, it's the *what, why,* and *how* for your stronger arms and upper body. Now you're ready to begin, not just to do it, but to do it right!

CHAPTER 2

Training Guidelines

You can expect a properly implemented resistance-training program to result in positive adaptations by the body's systems, including the cardiorespiratory, immunoendocrinological, skeletal, connective tissue, and neuromuscular. Such a resistance-training program begins with the overload principle.

The overload principle is basic to training and a fundamental tenet in exercise physiology. According to it, during resistance training a greater amount of load is placed on the body than it is generally accustomed to. This overload results in the body's systems adapting or changing to accommodate the greater stress and load.

A caveat to the overload principle is important to mention here: to successfully implement a training program, regardless of your specific goals, you should keep in mind that the body will eventually adjust to predictable workloads and no longer adapt. When this adaptation process ceases, if greater stresses or loads are not placed on the system, the body starts to lose the initial benefits of the resistance program.

Does this mean you'll eventually be bench pressing buildings to sustain positive adaptation? Not at all! By changing resistance protocols among free weights, machines, and bodywork—by altering training variables and mixing up positions and movements—you can sustain positive adaptation. Once a fitness level is optimized, it can be maintained indefinitely at 70 percent of whatever work it took to get there by mixing up the training regimens you use. And you'll enjoy your workouts more, since you thereby avoid monotonous overtraining and neural stagnation.

How the Body Adapts to Resistance Training

This chapter is about the general adaptations of the body to resistance training. After we briefly discuss how the body adapts to resistance training, we present training guidelines and variables and we outline specific training adaptations.

Muscle Tissue

Hypertrophy is the change that occurs in muscle tissue as you implement resistance training. When you place stress on the musculature, the muscle fibers themselves accommodate it by increasing in size over a period of time. Resistance training does not increase the number of muscle fibers within a specific muscle. Rather, it causes an increase in the *size* of each single muscle fiber.

You cannot develop new muscle fibers as a result of weight training, but you can increase the size of the existing ones in your body. Hypertrophy specifically causes an increase in the cross-sectional area of each muscle fiber and increases the number of myofibrils within each fiber.

Connective Tissue

Tendons and ligaments, or connective tissue, also adapt to resistance training over time. Connective tissue is primarily composed of collagen fibers. The infrastructure of these fibers makes them strong and resistant to tearing. Elastin is a second component of connective tissue. It allows for a certain amount of stretch and range of motion in and around skeletal joints. Resistance training over time causes a general increase in the number, diameter, and density of collagen fibers. Elastin levels increase, proportionate to the gain in muscle strength, to maintain joint integrity.

Bone

The skeletal system adapts to resistance training through a process called *bone molding.* The loads that affect muscle and connective tissue also affect bone tissue over time through a process of cell transfer where fibers are mineralized, increasing the bone's density and diameter. In other words, the skeletal system builds greater resistance capabilities to the forces of a training program.

Obviously, all these bodily adaptations are adversely affected by improper training or long lapses in training. Metabolic enhancements also impede functional adaptations if they are ingested without proper training protocols. Adaptations that occur out of physiological sequence, or an appropriate time frame, are just as threatening to the health as having no adaptation at all.

This leads us to focusing the resistance training on improving the musculature system to benefit a particular need or goal. Let's first define these elements.

Components of Strength Training

There are four components to strength training, and the body can be trained to improve an individual in each of them: muscular strength, endurance, power, and balance. We next look at these components separately. Keep in mind, however, that the body can use the parameters by training a single component, two components, or all of them.

Bodybuilders, fitness enthusiasts, and athletes should all have an understanding of muscular strength, endurance, power, and balance. Consider the differences, however, among these three categories of people. Fitness enthusiasts have a different set of training goals than do bodybuilders or athletes. Their primary goals are general fitness and wellness. They will use moderate intensities, volumes, and loads during training, and they will strive for muscular balance and seek to avoid injury.

Bodybuilders, like fitness enthusiasts, are training for general muscular development. On the other hand, bodybuilders are looking to develop larger muscles with symmetrical balance. The only real difference between fitness enthusiasts and bodybuilders is that bodybuilders train with greater loads, volumes, and at higher intensities.

Athletes, compared with bodybuilders and fitness enthusiasts, work in a completely different situation. They train the body to perform specific movements within a sport. In other words, athletes train to the specificity of their sports, and they may not be so concerned with muscular size or symmetry. An athlete should begin by analyzing the sport and determining the required body positions and movements to be performed. From this awareness the athlete can determine what areas of the body to focus on in training and how to go about the training. The individual first determines whether muscular endurance, strength, or power is needed in the particular sport. Keep in mind the points made about fitness enthusiasts, bodybuilders, and athletes as you read these next sections and the rest of the book. We will add detail in later chapters on how to train for these bodybuilding, fitness, and athletic categories.

Muscular Strength

Muscles have the ability to produce maximum force at a given point in time, which is called *strength*. Resistance training is useful to develop strength. It focuses on selecting particular exercises, performing specified repetitions for each exercise, and using specific amounts of weight for each lift.

As a general rule, however, when training for muscular strength, you select and use a weight you can lift between 8 and 12 repetitions per set.

Muscular Endurance

The ability of the muscles to produce force over time is referred to as *muscular endurance*. This is what allows a muscle to continuously contract over an extended amount of time.

Training for muscular endurance usually involves a program implementing high-repetition exercises in the specific muscular system you are training. Resistance programs geared toward endurance training focus on 15 or more repetitions per set of a given exercise.

Power

Power is strength plus speed, or the ability of the muscle to produce a maximum amount of force in a given amount of time. Power refers to performing a movement in a specified amount of time or the shortest time possible, usually aiming for the latter.

Individuals who train for power attempt to lift large amounts of weight in an explosive and rapid manner. Power training has very low levels of repetitions, usually three to five repetitions per set of a given exercise.

Muscular Balance

To have muscular balance requires "hypertrophic parity." This refers to an equilibrium in the body's ratios of strength to endurance, to power, and to flexibility in an individual's work or play environment.

Training for balance requires performing reps and sets (to tolerance) that address the various agonist, antagonist, and synergist muscles proportionately. It's an integration, rather than an isolation, of these muscles. The *agonists* are the muscles directly involved in creating concentric skeletal movement. They are also referred to as prime movers. For example, the biceps is the prime mover or agonist in a biceps curl. The *antagonists* are the muscles that counter the contraction of an agonist in a skeletal movement. In the example of the biceps curl, for instance, the triceps is an antagonist. The *synergists*, also referred to as secondary movers, are those muscles involved indirectly in the movement. They support the agonists and antagonists as they initiate skeletal movement.

We strongly emphasize this element of balance with all our clients. The protocols require extra sets and reps using the less "glamorous" muscles. These less glamorous muscles are the muscles that primarily function as synergists or secondary movers. Some examples of such muscles are the rotator cuff muscles (supraspinatus, infraspinatus, teres minor, and subscapularis), the rhomboids, and the erector spinae of the back. Training these muscles is well worth the effort. It rewards you with more efficient strength plus reduced risk of injury!

To summarize, the body may be trained to improve in one specific area or with a combination of strength, endurance, power, and balance.

Training Variables

Each type of training carries its own amounts of repetitions and weights to attain specific improvement. And there are other modifications, called *training variables*, possible within each type of training.

Five specific training variables are associated with resistance work and can be modified to change the outcome of conditioning protocols. Each of the training elements uses these variables to achieve a specific outcome. The training variables are load, intensity, volume, duration, and frequency. Let's identify the contribution of each variable.

Load

Load refers to the amount of weight you use for each repetition. The load will vary from exercise to exercise and from person to person.

There is no baseline rule to follow in regard to specific load settings for certain exercises. The amount is determined completely on an individual basis.

Intensity

Intensity is the power output for an exercise (ranging from 0 percent to 100 percent), or the work per unit of time (load and speed of movement). An exercise's intensity is best equated in terms of a percentage of an individual's one-repetition maximum (1RM). Muscular endurance, strength, and power all are set at differing levels of intensity.

You can find information provided here to help you determine your 1RM in certain exercises, which in turn will equate with certain intensity levels.

Volume

The training variable of volume refers to the total amount of weight lifted in an exercise (load × repetitions). For example, if you perform three sets of the bench press using a load of 200 pounds, and lift 5 times for each set, your total volume for that exercise would be 3,000 pounds. Volume can be equated for a single set, for a training session, or for multiple training sessions.

If you observed different participants involved in resistance training, in general you would see large amounts of volume being lifted by bodybuilders and strength athletes (e.g., football players, Olympic lifters) in their attempting to increase muscular size and strength. On the other hand, among endurance athletes (e.g., swimmers, triathletes) and fitness enthusiasts, who have different goals, you would see individuals tending to lift less in terms of volume.

Duration

The amount of time between each exercise set is referred to as duration. This training variable is important to clarify: we're talking about the *rest interval* between sets of an exercise. It is not the amount of time spent performing a specific lift. Think about this. If you perform three sets of biceps curls with a rest time of one minute, and at the next workout you perform the same exercise with a rest time of 30 seconds, you have then worked the muscle harder because of the shorter rest period.

Frequency

The final training variable is frequency, or how often you work out. In general, bodybuilders train more frequently than do fitness enthusiasts. Athletes train just as often as bodybuilders—or even more—but spend more time on sport-specific activities. Fitness enthusiasts tend to spend less time actually participating in resistance-training activities than the other two categories, but these are only general statements.

The training variables can be modified as a group or individually to increase the overall intensity of your workout. You might increase the load of each set, for example, or increase both the load and intensity of each exercise. All five of these variables are conducive to improving your schedule of resistance training. The point is that adjustments in one or all of them can be beneficial to your resistance training. Understand each variable and determine how it comes into play when training for muscular strength, endurance, power, and balance. Guidelines for how these variables come into play when determining the proper load, volume, intensity, frequency, and duration are quite simple. Please review the information about muscular hypertrophy, endurance, and power to get a quick idea on how to adjust each variable.

Using the One-Repetition Maximum

Table 2.1 contrasts two kinds of amount: *repetition maximum* (RM), or the number of reps that can be performed with a load, compared with *one-repetition maximum (1RM),* or the most weight a person can lift once. This table and how you use it will help set the foundation for your choice of training program.

All resistance work takes place in the zone between a person's repetition maximum and a person's one-repetition maximum. Understand that this table is used to determine *both* your 1RM and your training zone. *Training zone* refers to what percentage of your 1RM you want to be training in to achieve your personal specified goals. Muscular endurance programs train at a much lower percentage of the 1RM than do strength-orientated training programs.

Table 2.1

DETERMINING RM AND 1RM

| % of 1RM: | 100.0 | 93.5 | 91.0 | 88.5 | 86.0 | 83.5 | 81.0 | 78.5 | 76.0 | 73.5 |
Repetitions:	1	2	3	4	5	6	7	8	9	10
Weight lifted (lb)	0.0	0.0	0.0	0.0	0.0	0.0	0.0	0.0	0.0	0.0
	5.0	4.7	4.5	4.4	4.3	4.2	4.1	3.9	3.8	3.7
	10.0	9.4	9.1	8.9	8.6	8.4	8.2	7.9	7.6	7.4
	15.0	14.0	13.7	13.3	12.9	12.5	12.2	11.8	11.4	11.0
	20.0	18.7	18.2	17.7	17.2	16.7	16.2	15.7	15.2	14.7
	25.0	23.4	22.8	22.1	21.5	20.9	20.2	19.6	19.0	18.4
	30.0	28.1	27.3	26.6	25.8	25.1	24.3	23.6	22.8	22.1
	35.0	32.7	31.9	31.0	30.1	29.2	28.4	27.5	26.6	25.7
	40.0	37.4	36.4	35.4	34.4	33.4	32.4	31.4	30.4	29.4
	45.0	42.1	41.0	39.8	38.7	37.6	36.5	35.3	34.2	33.1
	50.0	46.8	45.5	44.3	43.0	41.8	40.5	39.3	38.0	36.8
	55.0	51.4	50.1	48.7	47.3	45.9	44.6	43.2	41.8	40.4
	60.0	56.1	54.6	53.1	51.6	50.1	48.6	47.1	45.6	44.1
	65.0	60.8	59.2	57.5	55.9	54.3	52.7	51.0	49.4	47.8
	70.0	65.5	63.7	62.0	60.2	58.5	56.7	55.0	53.2	51.5
	75.0	70.1	68.3	66.4	64.5	62.6	60.8	58.9	57.0	55.1
	80.0	74.8	72.8	70.8	68.8	66.8	64.8	62.8	60.8	58.8
	85.0	79.5	77.4	75.2	73.1	71.0	68.9	66.7	64.6	62.5
	90.0	84.2	81.9	79.7	77.4	75.2	72.9	70.7	68.4	66.2
	95.0	88.8	86.5	84.1	81.7	79.3	77.0	74.6	72.2	69.8

	93.5	91.0	88.5	86.0	83.5	81.0	78.5	76.0	73.5
100.0	93.5	91.0	88.5	86.0	83.5	81.0	78.5	76.0	73.5
105.0	98.2	95.6	92.9	90.3	87.7	85.1	82.4	79.8	77.2
110.0	102.9	100.1	97.4	94.6	91.9	89.1	86.4	83.6	80.9
115.0	107.5	104.7	101.8	98.9	96.0	93.2	90.3	87.4	84.5
120.0	112.2	109.2	106.2	103.2	100.2	97.2	94.2	91.2	88.2
125.0	116.9	113.8	110.6	107.5	104.4	101.3	98.1	95.0	91.9
130.0	121.6	118.3	115.1	111.8	108.6	105.3	102.1	98.8	95.6
135.0	126.2	122.9	119.5	116.1	112.7	109.4	106.0	102.6	99.2
140.0	130.9	127.4	123.9	120.4	116.9	113.4	109.9	106.4	102.9
145.0	135.6	132.0	128.3	124.7	121.1	117.5	113.8	110.2	106.6
150.0	140.3	136.5	132.8	129.0	125.3	121.5	117.8	114.0	110.3
155.0	144.9	141.1	137.2	133.3	129.4	125.6	121.7	117.8	113.9
160.0	149.6	145.6	141.6	137.6	133.6	129.6	125.6	121.6	117.6
165.0	154.3	150.2	146.0	141.9	137.8	133.7	129.5	125.4	121.3
170.0	159.0	154.7	150.5	146.2	142.0	137.7	133.5	129.2	125.0
175.0	163.6	159.3	154.9	150.5	146.1	141.8	137.4	133.0	128.6
180.0	168.3	163.8	159.3	154.8	150.3	145.8	141.3	136.8	132.3
185.0	173.0	168.4	163.7	159.1	154.5	149.9	145.2	140.6	136.0
190.0	177.7	172.9	168.2	163.4	158.7	153.9	149.2	144.4	139.7
195.0	182.3	177.5	172.6	167.7	162.8	158.0	153.1	148.2	143.3
200.0	187.0	182.0	177.0	172.0	167.0	162.0	157.0	152.0	147.0
205.0	191.7	186.6	181.4	176.3	171.2	166.1	160.9	155.8	150.7
210.0	196.4	191.1	185.9	180.6	175.4	170.1	164.9	159.6	154.4
215.0	201.0	195.7	190.3	184.9	179.5	174.2	168.8	163.4	158.0
220.0	205.7	200.2	194.7	189.2	183.7	178.2	182.7	167.2	161.7

(continued)

Table 2.1 (continued)

% of 1RM: Repetitions:	100.0 1	93.5 2	91.0 3	88.5 4	86.0 5	83.5 6	81.0 7	78.5 8	76.0 9	73.5 10
Weight lifted (lb)	225.0	210.4	204.8	199.1	193.5	187.9	182.3	176.6	171.0	165.4
	230.0	215.1	209.3	203.6	197.8	192.1	186.3	180.6	174.8	169.1
	235.0	219.7	213.9	208.0	202.1	196.2	190.4	184.5	178.6	172.7
	240.0	224.4	218.4	212.4	206.4	200.4	194.4	188.4	182.4	176.4
	245.0	229.1	223.0	216.8	210.7	204.6	198.5	192.3	186.2	180.1
	250.0	233.8	227.5	221.3	215.0	208.8	202.5	196.3	190.0	183.8
	255.0	238.4	232.1	225.7	219.3	212.9	206.6	200.2	193.8	187.4
	260.0	243.1	236.6	230.1	223.6	217.1	210.6	204.1	197.6	191.2
	265.0	247.8	241.2	234.5	227.9	221.3	214.7	208.1	201.4	194.8
	270.0	252.5	245.7	239.0	232.2	225.5	218.7	212.0	205.2	198.5
	275.0	257.1	250.3	243.4	236.5	229.6	222.8	215.9	209.0	202.1
	280.0	261.8	254.8	247.8	240.8	233.8	226.8	219.8	212.8	205.8
	285.0	266.5	259.4	252.2	245.1	238.0	230.9	223.7	216.6	209.5
	290.0	271.2	263.9	256.7	249.4	242.5	234.9	227.7	220.4	213.2
	295.0	275.9	268.5	261.1	253.7	246.3	239.0	231.6	224.2	216.8
	300.0	280.5	273.0	265.5	258.0	250.5	243.0	235.5	228.0	220.5
	305.0	285.2	277.6	269.9	262.3	254.7	247.1	239.4	231.8	224.2
	310.0	289.9	282.1	274.4	266.6	258.9	251.1	243.4	235.6	227.9
	315.0	294.5	286.7	278.8	270.9	263.0	255.2	247.3	239.4	231.5
	320.0	299.2	291.2	283.2	275.2	267.2	259.2	251.2	243.2	235.2
	325.0	303.9	295.8	287.6	279.5	271.4	263.3	255.1	247.0	238.9

330.0	308.6	300.3	292.1	283.8	275.9	267.3	259.1	250.8	242.6
335.0	313.2	304.9	296.5	288.1	279.7	271.4	263.0	254.6	246.2
340.0	317.9	309.4	300.9	292.4	283.9	275.4	266.9	258.4	249.9
345.0	322.6	314.0	305.3	296.7	288.1	279.5	270.8	262.2	253.6
350.0	327.3	318.5	309.8	301.0	292.3	283.6	274.8	266.0	257.3
355.0	331.9	323.1	314.2	305.3	296.4	287.6	278.7	269.8	260.9
360.0	336.6	327.6	318.6	309.6	300.6	291.6	282.6	273.6	264.6
365.0	341.3	332.2	323.0	313.9	304.8	295.7	286.5	277.4	268.3
370.0	346.0	336.7	327.5	318.2	309.0	299.7	290.5	281.2	272.0
375.0	350.6	341.3	331.9	322.5	313.1	303.8	294.4	285.0	275.6
380.0	355.3	345.8	336.3	326.8	317.3	307.8	298.3	288.8	279.3
385.0	360.0	350.4	340.7	331.1	321.5	311.9	302.2	292.6	283.0
390.0	364.7	354.9	345.2	335.4	325.7	315.9	306.2	296.4	286.7
395.0	369.3	359.5	349.6	339.7	329.8	320.0	310.1	300.2	290.3
400.0	374.0	364.0	354.0	344.0	334.0	324.0	314.0	304.0	294.0
405.0	378.7	368.6	358.4	348.3	338.2	328.1	317.9	307.8	297.7
410.0	383.4	373.1	362.9	352.6	342.4	332.1	321.9	311.6	301.4
415.0	388.0	377.7	367.3	356.9	346.5	336.2	325.8	315.4	305.0
420.0	392.7	382.2	371.7	361.2	350.7	340.2	329.7	319.2	308.7
425.0	397.4	386.8	376.1	365.5	354.9	344.3	333.6	323.0	312.4
430.0	402.1	391.3	380.6	369.8	359.1	348.3	337.6	326.8	316.1
435.0	406.7	395.9	385.0	374.1	363.2	352.4	341.5	330.6	319.7
440.0	411.4	400.4	389.4	378.4	367.4	356.4	345.4	334.4	323.4
445.0	416.1	405.0	393.8	382.7	371.6	360.5	349.3	338.2	327.1
450.0	420.8	409.5	398.3	387.0	375.8	364.5	353.3	342.0	330.8
455.0	425.4	414.1	402.7	391.3	379.9	368.6	357.2	345.8	334.4

Determining Repetition Maximum and One-Repetition Maximum

Determining your RM is a relatively simple task if you are experienced and well rested. However, beginning trainees sometimes have not developed the skill, balance, and other neurological attributes that would allow for a safe and effective RM testing procedure.

Regardless of your experience level, *always use a spotter* when determining your 1RM. A spotter prevents the possibility of injury and also aids in providing an accurate test result. In the early stages of training it may be appropriate to use a higher RM value or more reps with a lighter weight.

Here's how to estimate 1RM from a 10RM test-measured value. You first perform a set of 10 repetitions with a light weight. Depending on the ease with which this is completed, add additional weight. The incremental increase in weight will be determined by the ease of the previous lift. For example, if you easily lift 225 pounds for 10 repetitions, your next increment would be large. On the other hand, if the 225-pound lift was difficult but nevertheless you achieved 10 repetitions, your next raise in weight would be small. Next you should perform another set of 10 repetitions. Allow a *rest* of two to four minutes between the trials to ensure adequate recuperation.

Continue the process until you discover a weight allowing only 10 repetitions. An experienced instructor can help you by supervising the process so that the 10RM value can be discovered in fewer than five trials. You can then consult table 2.1 and find in the 10-repetition column of the table the weight you achieved, then find the weight on the same line in the 1RM column to estimate your 1RM. For example, 10 repetitions with 305 pounds yields a 1RM of 415 pounds.

The formula for the 1RM works for all individuals and athletes. It does not change if you are a bodybuilder or football player: the equation and results remain the same.

In a start-up training regimen you should perform exercises at a repetition level of 8 to 10, use the 1RM table to determine your one-rep max at 100-percent intensity, and then proceed to calculate the repetition levels necessary to reach specific program goals.

Accuracy

These tables have stirred some controversy as to their accuracy for different athletes and different lifts. They seem to be more accurate for free-weight and multiple-joint exercises than for machine exercises. They are intended to provide a general guide until the trainee has developed the neural and proprioceptive skills and attributes that make testing at low RMs (that is, 1RM to 5RM) safe and effective.

Rep Levels and Load Assignments

Different repetition levels result in different training outcomes. Rep levels and load assignments (that is, the percentage of 1RM) are linked. Although this is an oversimplification, the following formulas may help you remember the relationship among repetitions, loads, and goals. High repetition, low intensity, and large volumes result in an increase in the *endurance* of a muscle. This type of repetition and load assignment would be ideal for an endurance athlete, such as a swimmer. It would also be appropriate for someone looking to increase the endurance of the muscular system.

Moderate repetition, moderate intensity, and moderate volumes result in increases in *strength* and *size* of the muscle. Bodybuilders who tend to train with moderate loads and repetition levels fit into this category. They are not concerned about the strength of the muscle, but rather its size and shape.

Low repetition, high intensity, and low volumes result in an increase in the *power output* of the muscle. Power lifters and other strength athletes (football players, track-and-field athletes) would be interested in training for both strength and movement speed. These types of individuals would look to train with low repetitions and high intensities. Mixing and matching the repetitions, intensity, and volumes to tolerance in the synergists results in balance. (See table 2.2 for a detailed integration of training types and training variables.)

Finally, you'll note that one of the training variables—volume—is not included in table 2.2. Volume is a dependent variable. Its quantification is a function of load, intensity, repetitions, sets, and workout frequency. Volume refers to the total amount of weight lifted in a given training session or sessions. It can also be defined as the total number of repetitions and the varying loads lifted within a training session. Volume can be computed as the weight, times the number of repetitions, times the sets performed in a given exercise: weight $\times$ reps $\times$ sets = volume.

For example, if you do the bench press with 200 pounds for 10 repetitions in 3 sets, the total volume for that exercise would be $200 \times 10 \times 3$, or 6,000 pounds. There is also an inverse relationship between intensity and volume. When the intensity or loads are high

Table 2.2

INTEGRATING TRAINING VARIABLES AND TYPE OF TRAINING

Training variable

Type of training	Load and intensity level	Per-set level (number) of repetitions	Between-set duration (seconds or minutes)	Workout frequency (times per week)
Strength/ hypertrophy	70%-90%	6-12	30-60 sec.	4
Endurance	70% or less	15 or more	Up to 60 sec.	2-6
Power	90% or more	5 or fewer	2-3 min.	2-3
Balance	90% or less	6 or more	2 min. or less	2-6

in a training regimen, the total volume of that training session will be low. When intensity or loads are low, the total volumes will be high.

Specific Training Adaptations

With your improved understanding of the variables within resistance training, let's revisit the principle of overload and the body's adaptations to resistance work. There are three possible outcomes for the body with overload and adaptation.

- Positive—when the training load placed on the body induces a positive adaptation or a gain in the level of fitness.
- Neutral—when the training load placed on the body induces no adaptation and there isn't a gain or a loss in the level of fitness.
- Negative—when the training load placed on the body induces a negative adaptation and there is a decrease in the level of fitness.

You can use two strategies to prevent accommodation: (1) you can maintain the same training program, but change the training variables load and intensity, or (2) you can change the stimuli by changing the training program.

Specificity and cross-specificity are training philosophies based on (specific) personal improvement goals or (cross-specific) work-play improvement goals. Baseline training programs are successful only when personalized to an individual's specific goals and objectives. We'll provide plenty of training options; you have the hard part now—identifying your needs and then committing to a specific program.

Muscle Recovery

Recovery and resistance training work hand and glove in both micro- and macrocycles. Everyone prepares, performs, and repairs in daily, weekly, monthly, and yearly cycles of work or play. Muscles fail. The muscle failure might be chemical (due to lactic acid) or physiological (due to microtears). Either way, the body must regenerate. Using metabolic enhancements can help (see chapter 10), but recovery time must be part of any resistance-training program. Let's look at some guidelines to use in determining recovery time.

Micro- and Macrocycles

In resistance training, recovery time can be discussed at the levels of a microcycle and macrocycle. The microcycle refers to the recovery time between sets and exercise during a workout. The recovery time in a microcycle can be determined by the specificity of your training. Table 2.3 describes the correct recovery times within a microcycle to use when training for power, strength, endurance, and balance.

Table 2.3
MICROCYCLE RECOVERY TIMES

Type of workout	Recovery time
Power	3-5 min.
Strength/hypertrophy	30-60 sec.
Endurance	30 sec. or 1:1 ratio work/rest interval
Balance	30-60 sec. or 1:1 ratio work/rest interval

Determining the Duration of Rest

Rest periods between microcycle workouts are critical to proper training. A few factors come into play when looking at recovery time. The first variable is what muscle is being trained.

Muscle size. Generally speaking, small muscles (for example, biceps and triceps) can be trained with less rest than larger muscles (for example, chest or back). A small muscle can be trained with only 24 hours' recovery time between workouts, whereas larger muscles may require a recovery time of 48 hours.

Load or intensity. Another factor in recovery time is the load-intensity levels in your program. Higher loads require greater recovery time between workouts than do workouts performed with submaximal loads. Normally, it is recommended that you allow a minimum of 72 hours for recovery when training with large loads.

Metabolism and seasonal training. A third factor, however, affects "normal" recovery. Metabolic enhancers and boosters (see chapter 10) are proving to significantly reduce recovery time in all training activities. Year-round training programs should sequence from microcycles to mesocycles to macrocycles, with active rest facilitating recovery in and between each cycle. Programs and cycles can also be "phased" according to the seasonal requirements of a particular sport, with preparing, peaking, and recovering times planned accordingly. For example, the training variables in weightlifting, shot-putting, tennis, baseball, and football, would be manipulated in different ways appropriate to athletes in these particular sports (see Fleck & Kramer, *Essentials of Strength Training*, Champaign, Illinois: Human Kinetics, 1994 for more information on planning cycles).

There's an important final note to remember on the concepts of phasing, cycling, and periodization. Don't let the routine become the ritual. *You* control your training regimen. Your training regimen doesn't control you. Listen to your arms and upper body as you implement a training program to achieve your goals, and both will tell you how well you've planned.

CHAPTER 3

Functional Flexibility

Think of functional flexibility as a total upper-body wake-up call. It's not "stretching" in the traditional sense, although some of the protocol looks like stretching. Instead, functional flexing asks muscle tissue, connective tissue, and joint tissue to "wake up" with isometric resistance in various positions that are *specific* to what people do in their everyday work or play. It becomes a *functionally integrated* exercise, therefore, not an isolation exercise. It creates a balanced warm-up for sequencing the strength and flexibility required in daily activities. Again, every joint, tendon, and ligament and every small, medium, and large muscle can be flexed through the ranges of motion (ROM) specific to your work or play environment.

This program is a synthesis of what we've researched, experienced, and applied as professional athlete-coaches. It also synthesizes what we've observed and learned working in the Pacific rim, where some 2,000 years of experience with position and movement have resulted in disciplines ranging from passive yoga to aggressive martial arts. It's interesting to note that Japanese citizens nationwide participate in daily, low-intensity variations of these positions and movements at home and in their workplaces. They call it the "morning stretch," and it's part of their cultural (and corporate) belief system, enhancing both their job productivity and quality of life.

Integrated Flexibility, or Push-Pull Stretching

It's worth repeating that the routine we recommend is not isolated stretching, although some traditional stretching positions are involved. The majority of positions and movements involve a "push-pull" action from the muscles supporting the connective tissues. This push-pull in a fixed position creates an isometric muscle contraction, which builds strength and balance while improving flexibility through ROM.

Integrated flexibility elevates the core body temperature, flushes the muscles and joints with blood and oxygen, and enhances a critical intrabody relationship—a balance between strength and endurance. It's also the only protocol in your training regimen in which hyperflexion or hyperextension (or both) should be allowed. Why? Because the push-pull isometric positions and movements of the integrated flexibility protocol are adjusted to *your tolerance,* balancing the functional exchange of energy among agonists, antagonists, and synergists. You'll be surprised at how many "hot spots" show up during the work, and how this pushing and pulling in various positions integrates the balance of muscle–connective tissue strength with muscle–connective tissue endurance.

Take your time as you review the illustrations and explanations in this chapter. There are a couple caveats.

- Be aware that, depending on intensity, integrated flexibility can be a workout in and of itself, as well as preparation for other upper-body training protocols.

- When performing each exercise, remember the importance of correct position and movement to shoulder and elbow ROM. We suggest you *use a mirror until you've mastered the kinesthetics.* Maintaining your repetitions (or time) to tolerance facilitates both muscle form and muscle function.

Saws

Position

Hold the elbows at 90 degrees.

Action

Do sawing movements, front to back, back to front.

Perform 3 to 5 seconds or reps.

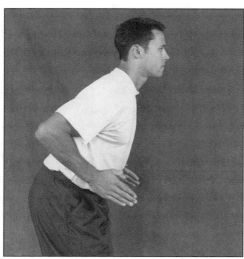

Saws

Position

Hold the elbows at 90 degrees.

Action

Do sawing movements, left to right, right to left.

Perform 3 to 5 seconds or reps.

Saws

Position

Hold the elbows at 90 degrees.

Action

1) Palms up, do sawing movements, the right hand over the left.

2) Palms down, do sawing movements, the right hand over the left.

Perform 3 to 5 seconds or reps.

1)

2)

The Flex-T Position Defined

Flex-T describes the elbow's position at shoulder height and slightly in front of the shoulder joints. It is a position of optimal joint integrity for the shoulders and elbows. The exercises you do in this position, which somewhat resembles how a baseball pitcher might hold his arms and shoulders, will improve flexibility in your shoulders.

Flex-T Why Me's

Position

Hold the arms and hands in a thumbs-level position (a). Note that the positions for this exercise are the same with or without dumbbells.

Action

Extend the forearm as in the photo, thumbs up (b), then in a thumbs-down position (c).

Perform one set of 3 to 5 reps per movement.

a)

Flex-T Why Me's *(continued)*

b)

c)

Flex-T Push-Pulls

The push-pull type of exercise can be isometric or isokinetic. Push, then pull, for three to five reps or seconds, to tolerance, as many times as you need to loosen up the muscles, tendons, and ligaments of your shoulders, elbows, forearms, and hands.

Position

Clasp the hands, holding the forearms and elbows at shoulder height.

Action

Push-pull with your elbows moving right and left.

Push-pull with your elbows moving in forward circles.

Push-pull with your elbows moving in backward circles.

Push-pull with your elbows moving in swim motions forward.

Push-pull with your elbows moving in swim motions backward.

Push-pull, doing press-downs and press-ups with your elbows touching in front of your chest.

Perform one set of 3 to 5 reps per movement.

Pull position

Push position

Flex-T Push-Pulls *(continued)*

Swims

Circles

Shoulder Shrugs

Using shoulder shrugs you can work in variations, combining them in *straight, circular, and swimming motions.*

Position

Standing, working the shoulders with shrugs.

Action

1) Shrug straight up and down.

2) Shrug forward and backward.

3) Shrug the shoulders and make circles forward.

4) Shrug the shoulders and make circles backward.

5) Shrug the shoulders and "swim" forward.

6) Shrug the shoulders and "swim" backward.

Perform one set of 3 to 5 reps per movement.

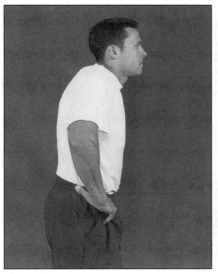

1)

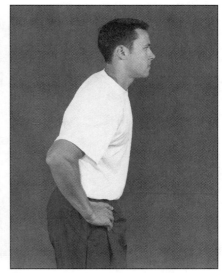

3)

OK, you have now elevated your core body temperature with some integrated flexibility; you are ready for some other protocols and to develop stronger arms and upper body. The next chapter addresses the specifics of how to prepare stability in the joints.

CHAPTER 4

Joint Stabilization

Joint integrity or stabilization work combines open-chain and closed-chain exercise protocols—positions and movements specific to creating stability in joint tissues and developing strength and endurance in the small and medium muscles, or synergists, surrounding the shoulders, elbows, and wrists. "Fine," you say, "but what the heck is an open-chain or closed-chain protocol, and why should I care about strength and endurance in my synergists?" The concepts of open- and closed-chain resistance are explained in the next few paragraphs. These concepts and applications are not new to researchers. They are, however, relatively new to the world of fitness. Fitness professionals have found it best to integrate both types into training. Elite or everyday athletes seldom break down in a prime mover (agonist or antagonist). They most often injure secondary movers (synergists) that facilitate or support joint movement. You might want to review the illustrations of muscle and connective tissue in chapter 1.

The Advantages
of Using Closed-Chain Exercise

It's a simplification, but think of open-chain resistance as isolated movements; an example, using machines, is doing a seated leg press. Think of closed-chain training, on the other hand, as integrated and coordinated movements that involve more than one joint; examples using the body's own weight would be a squat, a lunge, a push-up, or balancing on one leg. The advantage of closed-chain exercising is that it is more like actual performance involving integrated muscular movements. Most actions are sequences of movements that involve the whole body. A squat for example uses the hips, knees, and ankles in sequence.

Closed-chain exercises require contact with the ground, whether with one or both hands or one or both feet. They develop prime movers but also stabilizer muscles at the joints. They can be sport-specific and are efficient. Open-chain exercises (e.g., arm curls or triceps extensions) do not require contact with the ground. They can build muscles but are less like everyday or sport motions.

Most bodybuilders focus especially on open-chain work and the prime movers, but every sport or fitness enthusiast should also implement joint stabilization workouts. If you've ever been diagnosed with shoulder impingement, tennis elbow, or carpal tunnel syndrome, for instance, you can appreciate the importance of building strength and endurance in your synergists. These synergists are essential muscles, which help you perform large numbers of repetitive movements during daily work or play.

The open-chain protocols we recommend later in this chapter involve repetitions performed with light dumbbells, elastic cords, and plyoballs, or medicine balls. The closed-chain protocols involve vertical and horizontal body positions and movements, where your body's weight provides the resistance to build the muscles' strength, endurance, and balance.

Bodywork, when taken only to tolerance, is low-risk resistance training. It can be isometric, where position only is attained and maintained for a particular duration or time frame. It can also be isotonic, where movement is added to position, in ROM of 90 degrees to 180 degrees. With bodywork, the resistance is the body's weight, a function of positioning your feet and belly button, or the center of gravity (CG). That is, on the vertical plane, with the feet directly below CG (i.e., a pull-up position) you use 100 percent of your body's weight. And on the horizontal plane, with the feet below the CG, you use 60 percent of the body's weight. With the feet even with the CG, you are using 80 percent body weight, and with the feet above the CG, you are using or involving 100 percent of body weight (i.e., a push-up position, with the hands on the ground and the feet on a box). With these approximations, repetitions can be quantified for volume. With bodywork, the level of tolerance is self-imposed. When you use free weights or machine work, shifting the body's position can allow a prime mover to get you another rep or two. Unlike free weights and machine work, however, the body (as it lifts the resistance) stops once a weak link is maxed out. Position or movement simply terminates itself.

We have found bodywork to be the fastest and *safest* training method available for building hypertrophic parity, or tissue balance with strength and endurance. Since there is little, if any, large-muscle failure, bodywork can be done daily, or scheduled around periodization with machine and free-weight work, again to tolerance. You can also build bulk by lifting your body, but it takes time and large repetitions. Ex-football star Herschel Walker built a very functional, muscular body without ever using machines or free weights, but he had the time to do hundreds of push-ups, chin-ups, dips, and so forth on a daily basis.

Finally, using bodywork for joint stabilization doesn't have to be done at a health club. Your body and some floor space are all you need, which means you have choices, not excuses. You can train at home, in your office, or in a hotel on the road. Notice that you "can" requires commitment and consistency, as well as convenience.

Closed-Chain Exercises

Here are some of the bodywork protocols we recommend. They involve closed-chain training that builds muscle strength and endurance using various body positions and movements.

1 Flex-T Butt-Ups

Butt-ups are flexibility exercises for stabilizing the elbow and shoulder joints.

Position

Sit on the floor with your back and legs straight.

Keep the head and shoulders forward and the elbows bent.

Action

Hold the hands next to your hips, facing 1) *forward*, 2) *backward*, 3) *inward*, and 4) *outward*, and lift the butt two or three inches, doing three to five reps in each hand position.

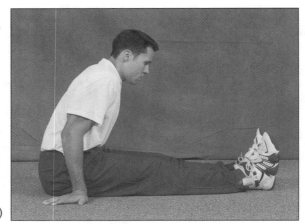
2)

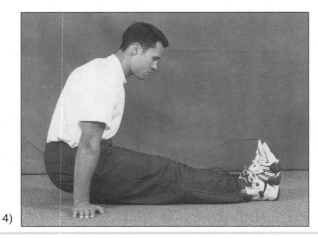
4)

2 Flex-T Push-Ups

You'll assume a basic Flex-T position on the floor, facing down. Do the Flex-T push-ups with the hands in three positions and the body working on three planes: incline (on a board or using a riser for the hands), horizontal (hands and feet on the floor), and decline (on a board or using a riser for the feet).

Position

Assume a basic push-up position, the elbows at shoulder-height in a Flex-T.

Action

1) Perform three to five push-ups with your hands in a neutral position.

2) Perform three to five push-ups with your hands supinated (the palms on the floor, facing your body).

3) Perform three to five push-ups with your hands pronated (the palms facing away from your body).

2)

2)

3 Side-Ups and One-Arm Push-Ups

Do the side-ups and one-arm push-ups in two hand positions.

Preparation

Lie on either side with your left or right forearm on the ground, placing your off hand 1) on your hip for body lifts and rotations, and 2) on the ground for push-ups.

Action

First raise your body up using the torso muscles. Hold, then move straight up and down, 1/2 hip turn straight up and down, then rotate your torso.

Perform 3 to 5 reps of each position and movement.

Second, with the hand on the ground, lean into it and press the body up using an extension of the arm; this will work the arm and shoulder stabilizer muscles.

Perform 3 to 5 reps.

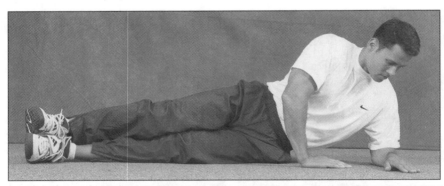

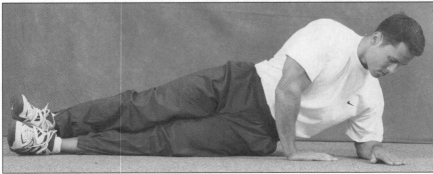

One-Arm Push-Ups

4 Elbow-Ups

Do the elbow-ups in four positions, with two movements. These exercises help stabilize the scapulae. Perform sets of three to five repetitions.

Position

Lying flat on the floor, belly-up, place your hands 1) on your thighs, 2) near your belly button, 3) with your thumbs in your arm pits, and 4) behind your head.

Action

Perform three to five elbow-ups, using your elbows to lift the shoulders and head off the floor.

Also, when you can do this movement comfortably, squeeze and pinch your shoulder blades together while your head and shoulders are raised.

1)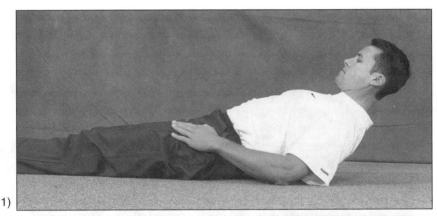

2)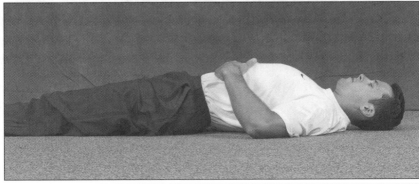

5 | Flex-T Cobra Shrugs

Do the Flex-T cobra shrugs in three positions, with two movements.

Position

Lying belly-down on the floor, lift your torso up slowly so that your weight rests on your forearms. Keep your belly button and lower body on the floor. You can think of yourself as a cobra about to strike!

Action

1) Take the cobra position and look straight ahead; shrug the shoulders back, pinching and unpinching the shoulder blades.

2) Take the cobra position and twist your head and torso to look right; shrug the shoulders back, pinching and unpinching the shoulder blades.

3) Take the cobra position and twist your head and torso to look left; shrug the shoulders back, pinching and unpinching the shoulder blades.

Perform 3 to 5 reps in each movement position.

1)

Open-Chain Exercises

Joint-stabilization work using open-chain protocols requires little, if any, introduction. Do the elastic cord work before work with the light dumbbells. The cord is a good complement to the dumbbells because it can give you isometric as well as isotonic work. Light dumbbells are 3 to 10 pounds in weight. Do as a single set per dumbbell exercise, with three to five reps per exercise angle.

Light dumbbells, elastic cords, and medicine balls are familiar to most people. We have, however, become much smarter in how to use them in training protocols. These exercises, when used as a *complement to bodywork* protocols given in the previous section, virtually guarantee strength and stamina in your synergists. The plyoball or medicine ball is great for postural stabilization, scapular stabilization, and high-elbow Flex-T reinforcement. It also helps build connective tissue and small muscle endurance.

Light Dumbbell Exercises

1 Shoulder Press

Preparation

Stand with the head forward of your belly button.

Feet shoulder-width apart, knees bent.

Dumbbells in hands; arms in a Flex-T position.

Action

Extend your arms so that they are slightly in front of and over your forehead (not exactly overhead).

1) Press *up* (palms straight).

2) Press up and rotate to palms facing *in*.

3) Press up and rotate to palms facing *out*.

Perform 3 to 5 reps with each position and movement.

Shoulder Press

1)

2)

3)

2 | Up Biceps—Down Triceps (Curls)

Preparation

Stand with the head forward of your belly button.

Feet shoulder-width apart, knees bent.

Dumbbells in hands; elbows always in front of the shoulder capsule.

Hold dumbbells at sides of body.

Action

Curl dumbbell up to palm at 1) *chest* level, 2) *shoulder* level, and 3) *ear* level, rotate to palm facing down, and lower dumbbell, alternating arms.

Perform 3 to 5 reps at each level.

1a)   1b)

Up Biceps–Down Triceps

2a)   2b)

3 Overhead Triceps Extension

Preparation

Stand with the head forward of your belly button.

Feet shoulder-width apart, knees bent.

Dumbbells in hands; elbows always in front of the shoulder capsule.

Hold weights above forehead.

Action

1) With the palms facing *each other,* extend dumbbells up and away from your head.

2) With the palms facing *forward,* extend dumbbells up and away from your head.

3) From the palms facing *out,* extend dumbbells up and away from your head.

Perform each movement 3 to 5 times.

1)   3)

4 Frontal Dumbbell Raises

Preparation

Stand with the head forward of your belly button.

Feet shoulder-width apart, knees bent.

Dumbbells in hands; elbows always in front of the shoulder capsule.

Hang the arms straight and in front of your belly button.

Action

With the palms facing *each other*, raise the dumbbells while holding your arms straight to shoulder level; lower back down with palms 1) *facing each other*, 2) *facing down*, and 3) *facing out*.

Perform each movement 3 to 5 times.

1)

2)

5 Hitchhikers (John Travoltas)

Preparation

Stand with the head forward of your belly button.

Feet shoulder-width apart, knees bent.

Dumbbells in hands; elbows always in front of the shoulder capsule.

Hang arms straight in front of belly button, thumbs down.

Action

1a) Raise the right arm above the head, and bend the elbow. The left arm stays in front of the pelvis and is slightly bent.

1b) Rotate the right arm to the position in front of the pelvis; simultaneously rotate the left arm up to the position above the head with the arm slightly bent.

Perform movement 9 to 15 times.

1a)   1b)

6   Flex-T Pulses

Preparation

Stand with the head forward of your belly button.

Feet shoulder-width apart, knees bent.

Dumbbells in hands; elbows in front of the shoulder capsule, in a Flex-T position, weights above the head.

Action

With the palms facing 1) *forward,* 2) *in*, and 3) *out*, pulse the dumbbells forward in small, rapid bursts to tolerance.

Perform movements 3 to 5 times in each position.

2)

3)

7 Scarecrows

Preparation

Stand with the head forward of your belly button.

Feet shoulder-width apart, knees bent.

Dumbbells in hands; elbows always in front of the shoulder capsule; arms hanging at sides, and weights resting on thighs.

Action

a) Palms facing backward, raise the elbows to a Flex-T, and extend forearms to a position above the head and stop.

b) Keep the elbows stable and lower the dumbbells to a position level with your shoulders, palms facing 1) forward, 2) in, and 3) out; pause for one second.

c) Lower the dumbbells to the starting position.

Perform 3 to 5 reps with each position and movement.

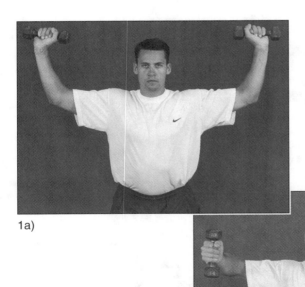

1a)

2b)

8 Dumbbell Flys

Preparation

Stand with the head forward of your belly button.

Feet shoulder-width apart, knees bent.

Dumbbells in hands; elbows always in front of the shoulder capsule.

Hold the dumbbells with the arms in front of your pelvis, the palms facing *in*.

Action

Raise the dumbbells together to shoulder level in an upright motion.

Extend the arms straight out to the sides.

Lower the dumbbells to starting position 1) keeping the palms facing in; 2) rotating the palms *back*, and 3) rotating the palms *forward* as you extend your arms.

Perform 3 to 5 reps with each position and movement.

Dumbbell Flys *(continued)*

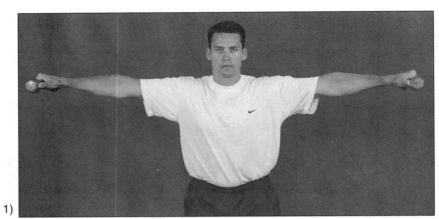

1)

2)

3)

9   Around the Worlds

Preparation

Stand with the head forward of your belly button.

Feet shoulder-width apart, knees bent.

Dumbbells in hands; elbows always in front of the shoulder capsule. Hold the dumbbells in front of your pelvis, with the palms facing *each other.*

Action

With the arms slightly bent, raise the dumbbells to above your forehead. 1) Keep your palms facing each other, 2) touch thumb to thumb at the top of the movement, and 3) touch the backs of your hands together at the top of the movement.

Lower the dumbbells to starting position.

Perform each movement 3 to 5 reps in each position.

1)

Around the Worlds *(continued)*

2)

3)

10 Bent-Over Lawn Mowers

Preparation

Stand with the head forward of your belly button.

Keep your feet wide, in a "power pyramid."

Lower your butt to a position between your legs.

Place the dumbbells on the floor.

From this power pyramid position, pick up the dumbbells.

Action

Alternate raising the right arm, then the left arm, into 1/2 a Flex-T position, palms 1) *facing in*, 2) *out*, and 3) *back*.

Perform movement 3 to 5 reps in each position.

Bent-Over Lawn Mowers *(continued)*

2)

3)

11 Bent-Over Flys

Preparation

Stand with the head forward of your belly button.

Keep your feet wide, in a "power pyramid."

Lower your butt to a position between your legs.

Place the dumbbells on the floor, your *palms* together and *facing each other*.

Action

a) Raise the dumbbells together to shoulder level in an upright motion.

b) Extend the arms straight out to the sides 1) palms *down*, 2) while rotating your palms *back*, and 3) while rotating your palms *forward*.

c) Lower the dumbbells to starting position.

Perform movement 3 to 5 reps in each position.

Bent-Over Flys *(continued)*

2b)

1b)

3b)

Elastic Cord Exercises

1 Shrugs

MUSCLES TRAINED: Shoulder capsule and rotator cuff

Preparation

Stand with both feet on the cord, the knees slightly bent. Your head should be over your belly button.

Hold the grips and cord with the arms extended, hands in four positions: palms facing forward, backward, in, and out.

Action

Keeping the arms extended, use the upper-body muscles to "shrug the shoulders" upward.

Lower and repeat.

Perform one set of 3 to 5 reps in each hand position.

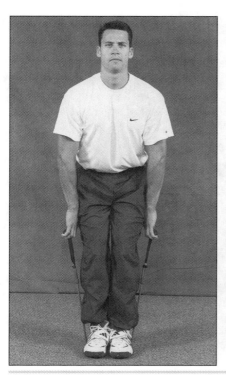 

2 Shoulder Circles

MUSCLES TRAINED: Shoulder capsule and rotator cuff

Preparation

Stand on the cord, feet together and knees slightly bent.

Your head should be over your belly button. Hold grips and cord with arms extended and hands facing backward.

Action

Circle shoulders forward.

Circle shoulders backward.

Perform one set of 3 to 5 reps per movement.

Circles backward

3 Shoulder Swims

MUSCLES TRAINED: Shoulder capsule and rotator cuff

Preparation

Stand on the cord, feet together and knees slightly bent.

Your head should be over your belly button. Hold grips and cord with arms extended and hands facing backward.

Action

Swim shoulders forward.

Swim shoulders backward.

Perform one set of 3 to 5 reps per movement.

Swims backward

4 Rotational Biceps Curls

MUSCLES TRAINED: Biceps and triceps

Preparation

Stand on the cord, feet together and knees slightly bent.

Your head should be over your belly button.

Hold the grips and cord with the arms extended.

Action

Curl right arm to shoulder level, palm up.

Rotate right hand to palm-down position, then return to the starting position.

Curl up left arm to shoulder level, palm up.

Rotate left hand to palm-down position, then return to the starting position.

Repeat.

Perform one set of 3 to 5 reps per movement.

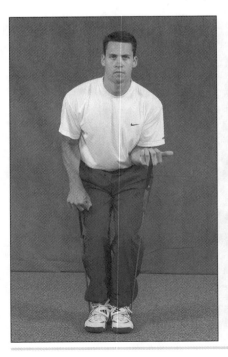 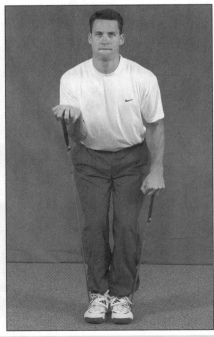

5 Flex-T Flys

MUSCLES TRAINED: Shoulder capsule and rotator cuff

Preparation

Stand with the feet on the cord and the knees bent.

Your head should be over your center of gravity.

Assume a Flex-T position with your arms.

Hold grips and cords with palms facing *in*.

Action

Lift elbows as high as possible (to tolerance), and pinch the scapulae together.

Maintain posture and elbow height and extend (fly) forearms sideways, forward, and backward.

Perform one set of 3 to 5 reps per movement.

6 Flex-T Swims Backward and Forward

MUSCLES TRAINED: Shoulder capsule and rotator cuff

Preparation

Stand with the feet shoulder-width apart and the knees bent.

Your head should be over your center of gravity.

Assume a Flex-T position with your arms.

Hold grips and cords a) thumbs level, b) thumbs up, and c) thumbs down.

Action

Swim forward.

Swim backward.

Perform one set of 3 to 5 reps per position and movement.

a)

Flex-T Swims Backward and Forward

c)

c)

7 Flex-T Hitchhikers Left and Right

MUSCLES TRAINED: Shoulder capsule and rotator cuff, arm flexors and extensors

Preparation

Stand with the feet shoulder-width apart and the knees bent.

Your head should be over your center of gravity.

Assume a Flex-T position with the arm you're not working.

Hold grips and cord firm and stable. With working arm, hold grip and cord in front of forehead, pointing thumb down.

Action

Extend the forearm back and up while you rotate the thumb *up*.

Return to the starting position.

Turn around and work the other arm.

Perform one set with 3 to 5 reps on both sides.

8 Flex-T Thumb Downs Left and Right

MUSCLES TRAINED: Shoulder capsule and rotator cuff, arm flexors and extensors

Preparation

Stand with the legs shoulder-width apart and the knees bent.

Assume a Flex-T position with the arm you're not working. Hold grip and cord firm and stable. With working arm, hold grip and cord thumb up in front of belly button.

Action

Extend forearm back and down while you rotate thumb down.

Return to starting position.

Turn around and work the other arm.

Perform one set of 3 to 5 reps on each side.

9 Reverse Arm Extensions

MUSCLES TRAINED: Shoulder capsule and rotator cuff, arm flexors and extensors

Preparation

Stand, facing away from wall or fence, feet shoulder-width apart and knees bent.

Your head should be over your belly button. Hold grips and cord with palms in and elbows at 90° and close to rib cage.

Action

Extend arms forward elbows first (until they get in front of torso) while rotating forearms into a thumbs-down position, then into a thumbs-up extension (like "Flex-T Why Me's" in bodywork).

Return to the starting position.

Perform one set of 3 to 5 reps.

10 Elbow Pulls

MUSCLES TRAINED: Shoulder capsule and rotator cuff, arm flexors

Preparation

Stand, feet shoulder-width apart and knees bent.

Your head should be over your belly button. Hold grips and cord with thumbs 1) up, 2) in, and 3) down. Elbows at 90° and close to rib cage.

Action

Pull the cord backward, maintaining elbow position.

Return to the starting position.

Perform one set with 3 to 5 reps in each position.

1)

1)

11 Triceps Extensions

MUSCLES TRAINED: Triceps, shoulder capsule and rotator cuff, arm extensors

Preparation

Stand, feet shoulder-width apart and knees bent.

Your head should be over your center of gravity. Hold grips and cord with thumbs up. Elbows at 90° and close to rib cage.

Action

Extend the arms downward while rotating the thumb *down* to a position behind the back. Return and repeat.

Perform one set of 3 to 5 reps.

Medicine Ball Exercises

1 Flex-T Wall Toss Wide Elbows

MUSCLES TRAINED: Shoulder capsule, rotator cuff, arm extensors and flexors

Preparation

Stand with the feet shoulder-width apart and the knees bent.

Keep the head resting comfortably over your center of gravity.

Place elbows wide on the wall.

Action

Grasp a medicine ball in the hands. Throw the medicine ball against the wall while your elbows remain touching the wall. Flexion of the arms occurs at the elbow.

As you throw the medicine ball in, a full flexion and extension of the arm occurs.

Perform one set of 45–60 tosses.

2   Flex-T Wall Toss Close Elbows

MUSCLES TRAINED: Shoulder capsule, rotator cuff, arm extensors and flexors

Preparation

Stand with the feet shoulder-width apart and the knees bent.

Keep the head over your center of gravity.

Place elbows next to your ears and on the wall.

Action

From the starting position, grasp a medicine ball in the hands.

Throw the medicine ball against the wall while your elbows remain touching the wall. Flexion of the arms occurs at the elbow.

Keep elbows close to the sides of your head. As you throw the medicine ball in, a full flexion and extension of the arm occurs.

Aim for 45–60 tosses.

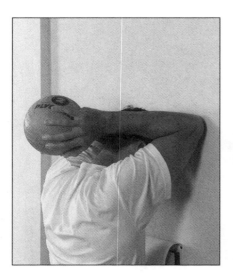 

3 Flex-T Right and Left Toss

MUSCLES TRAINED: Shoulder capsule, rotator cuff, arm extensors and flexors

Preparation

Stand with the feet shoulder-width apart and the knees bent.

Keep the head over your center of gravity.

Face the wall, standing about 8 to 12 inches away from it, in a perpendicular position with the medicine ball in hand.

Your toss elbow should be at shoulder level, and your other elbow should be in a Flex-T position.

Action

From starting position, throw and hold the medicine ball off the wall while your elbow remains at shoulder level. Extension of the arms occurs at the elbow.

Switch arms, and repeat the exercise.

Perform one set of 45–60 tosses.

This concludes part I, giving you information and instruction on building a strength foundation. In part II we provide specific machine and free-weight training protocols for stronger arms and upper body.

PART II
CORE
EXERCISES

This second part of *Stronger Arms and Upper Body* deals with specific machine and free-weight exercises for the chest, upper back, shoulders, biceps, triceps, forearms, wrists, and hands. Sport applications are prominent here, as are general fitness applications and bodybuilding. We also combine exercises for rehabilitation as well as "prehabilitation." This portion is purely instructional; it provides photos of and explanations and directions for core arm and upper body exercises.

Human movement and the physical preparation for human movement are the same for elite athletes as they are for recreational athletes, bodybuilders, and people pursuing fitness activity. Genetics and intensity are the only real differences that come into play, and these vary in good measure according to the requirements of an individual's work or play environment. So follow the logic: if you are successful and healthy in your work and play, you are evidently moving properly and are functionally fit. However, if you are not successful or if you are hurting in your work or play, something is amiss.

The protocols for arm and upper-body resistance training on machines and free weights that we present in chapters 5 through 9 will prepare and repair you, with form and function, for *any* work or play activity. All you have to do to personalize the protocol is match your own required level of fitness to the movements and workloads required by your individual work or play environment.

Chest

Chapter 5 presents you with a list of exercises focused on training the chest region. Remember that the chest region is composed entirely of the pectoralis major muscle. The pectoralis major mainly functions to extend and flex the shoulder joint. Secondary functioning of the pectoralis major is rotation and adduction of the shoulder joint. In chapter 1 we discussed this muscle as three separate sections: the upper, middle, and lower. The exercises in this chapter will focus either on the entire pectoralis major muscle or on a specified area.

Many athletic movements call upon the pectoralis major. Any biomechanical movement that results in an extension, flexion, adduction, or medial rotation of the shoulder joint, in fact, will draw on the chest muscles. Some examples of such actions include the execution of a swing in baseball, the catching of a pass in football, or the pulling of a paddle stroke in rowing. Any of these movements incorporates the pectoralis major.

When it comes to bodybuilding, overall development of the chest is of number-one importance, and the same holds true with the general fitness enthusiast. If you understand what movements your sport entails, or what goals you have as a bodybuilder or fitness enthusiast, you can pick and choose the exercises that correlate to the requirements of your sport.

If you experience pain—whether playing tennis or tiddlywinks, on the golf course or in the office, in the pool or on the couch—your body is telling you something is wrong. Hello! Your body's not dumb. Let it show you its smarts. . . . Listen to it! You might be experiencing repetitive movement trauma by doing some motion to excess; your motion might be inefficient; your functional strength might need remedial work—or all three.

If you fix the problem *before* you get hurt, we call it *prehabilitation*. The "fix" itself, however, is the same in prehabilitation and rehabilitation! How do you stay in "prehab" and avoid rehab? Here's a sequence in exercise physiology you should be aware of to match your work or play activity with your fitness level.

1. Activity leads to **stiffness** (the result of stressing muscle and connective tissue), which goes away in warm-up and eventually disappears completely with accommodation.

2. Activity leads to **soreness** (also the result of stressing muscle and connective tissue), which doesn't go away in warm-up, impedes but doesn't stop activity, and gets worse with intensity.

3. Activity leads to **injury** (also a result of stressing muscle, connective tissue, and bone), which should alert you to **stop the activity** until you are healed.

Before you begin the exercises in chapter 5, here are a few notes about them. You'll find both free-weight and machine-oriented exercises in this chapter. There is a noteworthy difference, however, between machine and free-weight exercises. Free-weight exercises tend to be more difficult because synergists are required to maintain balance of the weight as you move it through the prescribed line of action. Machines, on the other hand, also can do the work of setting your body in a prescribed position; they allow your muscles only to direct the weight in a single plane of action.

Both free weights and machines have advantages and disadvantages. For example, because machines set your body in the prescribed movement pattern, they tend to be easier for beginners. Free weights tend to recruit more muscles into the movement because of the requirement of stabilizing the body during the exercise. Machines, on the other hand, can create more specificity in an exercise because they can direct the focus to only one muscle.

The decision to use free weights or machines is up to you. We suggest you determine what your goals are and what your sport or bodybuilding goal requires, and go from there. Develop your program from this central idea, however: it is smart for beginners, or for advanced lifters using heavy weights, to *use a spotter to prevent injury.* It is better to be safe than injured.

1 Flat Bench Barbell Press

MUSCLES TRAINED: Pectorals

Preparation

Lie flat on the bench, with your hands from six inches to elbow width apart, but always wider than your shoulders (the Flex-T position!) and feet flat on the floor.

Action

Lower the bar to where elbows are at shoulder height.

Press the barbell to an arms-extended position, just short of locking out.

Keep the back flat, and do not bounce the weight on your chest.

Perform 1 to 3 sets of 3 to 12 reps to tolerance.

2 Flat Bench Dumbbell Flys

MUSCLES TRAINED: Pectorals

Preparation

Lie flat on the bench, your feet on the floor and the arms extended.

Hold the dumbbells in the hands, with the palms facing each other.

Action

Extend forearms and lower the dumbbells down to where elbows are shoulder height.

Press the dumbbells up to an arms-extended position, just short of locking out.

Return to starting position.

Perform 1 to 3 sets of 3 to 12 reps to tolerance.

3 Decline Bench Dumbbell Press

MUSCLES TRAINED: Lower pectorals

Preparation

Lie on a decline bench, with your feet or legs anchored.

Action

Hold the dumbbells in your hands, with the palms facing forward.

Lower the dumbbells down to where elbows are shoulder height.

Press the dumbbells up to an arms-extended position, just short of locking out.

Perform 1 to 3 sets of 3 to 12 reps to tolerance.

4 Cable Crossover Flys

MUSCLES TRAINED: Inner pectorals

Preparation

With the feet staggered in position, lean your body slightly forward.

Action

Hold the palms facing inward, the arms extended and elbows shoulder height and slightly bent.

Press the cable handles forward, your arms extending and the hands crossing in front of your belly button.

Return to the starting position.

Perform 1 to 3 sets of 3 to 12 reps to tolerance.

5 Incline Barbell Bench Press

MUSCLES TRAINED: Upper pectorals

Preparation

Lie on an incline bench with your hands from six inches to elbow-width apart, but always wider than your shoulders (the Flex-T position) and your feet flat on the floor.

Action

Lower the bar to comfort, without touching chest.

Press the barbell to an arms-extended position, just short of locking out.

Perform 1 to 3 sets of 3 to 12 reps to tolerance.

6 Incline Bench Dumbbell Press

MUSCLES TRAINED: Upper pectorals

Preparation

Lie on an incline bench, feet on the floor, dumbbells in a Flex-T position and palms facing forward.

Action

Palms forward, lower the dumbbells to the sides of your chest.

Extend your arms until the weights touch 1) palms forward, 2) palms in, and 3) palms out, and return to the starting position.

Perform 1 to 3 sets of 3 to 12 reps in each palm position.

7 Decline Bench Dumbbell Flys

MUSCLES TRAINED: Lower pectorals

Preparation

Lie on a decline bench, with the feet or legs anchored.

Hold dumbbells in your hands, palms facing inward.

Action

Extend forearms and lower dumbbells until the elbows are at shoulder height.

Press the dumbbells up to an arms-extended position, just short of locking out.

Return to the starting position.

Perform 1 to 3 sets of 3 to 12 reps to tolerance.

8 | Flat Bench Dumbbell Press

MUSCLES TRAINED: Pectoral group

Preparation

Lie flat on the bench, feet flat on the floor.

Hold dumbbells above the chest, palms forward.

Action

Extend the arms, your palms 1) forward, 2) rotating in, and 3) rotating out, touching at the top.

Return the arms to the starting position.

Perform 1 to 3 sets of 3 to 12 reps to tolerance.

Shoulders

Chapter 6 provides a series of exercises for the shoulder area, whose muscles generate many movements. The functions of the deltoid are adduction, abduction, extension, and flexion, as well as the medial and lateral rotation of the upper arm.

A quick review of the shoulder's anatomy tells us that the three heads of the shoulder's main muscle agonists (frontal deltoid, rear deltoid, and lateral deltoid head) and the antagonists (upper back and serratus) are used in many muscular actions. The exercises you find in this chapter are oriented to the prime movers. You probably can remember, or surmise, that the synergists (muscles that are indirectly involved and that support the agonist in skeletal movement) are also involved in the shoulder region's movements.

The primary synergists in the shoulder region are the four muscles of the rotator cuff, which are called the teres minor, supraspinatus, infraspinatus, and subscapularis. To avoid injury and to maintain a good strength ratio among agonist, antagonist, and synergist muscles, you must train all these muscles. We highly recommend that *prior to* any prime-mover shoulder work you perform the proper range-of-motion, flexibility, and joint-stabilization exercises. And it is well worth your reviewing both the information and exercises for ROM, flexibility, and stabilization before proceeding.

The bottom line is that before you begin any upper body prime-mover exercises, first do the proper facilitation of range-of-motion, flexibility, and joint-stabilization work. This provides you with a proper warm-up, helps prevent injury, and develops the appropriate ratios of muscular balance in the system.

Before we delve into the shoulder exercises, let's take a look at what kinds of athletic actions would involve the muscles of the shoulder. First, any striking or throwing of an object creates tremendous amounts of rotational torque from this area of the body. Striking a volleyball, swinging a bat, or throwing a football all require flexion, extension, and rotation of the shoulder region.

If you're an athlete looking to improve performance in your sport, you would do well to review the biomechanical actions used in your sport. Once you have reviewed the biomechanical actions, determine what exercises are cross-specific (that is, match the movements in your sport), and choose the exercise most suitable to improve your performance. If you're a fitness enthusiast or bodybuilder, you would look to develop muscular balance in the shoulder region and perhaps size as well.

In chapter 5 we discussed the advantages, disadvantages, and differences between using machines and free weights for exercise, and these observations hold true for working with the shoulder area as well. As with chest exercises, here again a spotter is recommended for beginners or exercisers using heavier loads.

One note of great importance is worth repeating: remember to do your range-of-motion, flexibility, and joint-stabilization exercises before proceeding to the prime-mover exercises!

1 Barbell Shoulder Press Behind the Neck

MUSCLES TRAINED: Deltoids (entire)

Preparation

Sit on the bench, with your back straight.

Grasp the bar with the hands at shoulder to elbow width in a Flex-T.

Action

Lower bar to touch the bottom of the neck.

Extend the arms to a position above the neck, just short of locking out.

Perform 1 to 3 sets of 3 to 12 reps to tolerance.

2 Seated Dumbbell Shoulder Press

MUSCLES TRAINED: Deltoids (entire)

Preparation

Sit on the bench, with your back straight.

Your elbows should be at shoulder level in a Flex-T with your palms facing forward.

Action

Press your arms to an extended position. Palms 1) forward, 2) rotating in, and 3) rotating out.

Lower the dumbbells to the starting position.

Perform 1 to 3 sets of 3 to 12 reps to tolerance.

3 Standing Dumbbell Side-Lateral Raises

MUSCLES TRAINED: Lateral deltoids

Preparation

Stand, with the feet shoulder-width apart or closer.

Place your arms at your sides, holding dumbbells, palms facing in.

Action

Raise the dumbbells up to shoulder height, keeping elbows slightly forward of shoulders.

Lower the dumbbells to your sides.

Perform 1 to 3 sets of 3 to 12 reps to tolerance.

4 Standing Frontal Dumbbell Raises

MUSCLES TRAINED: Frontal deltoids

Preparation

Stand, with the feet shoulder-width apart or closer.

Hold the dumbbells, palms down, resting on the thighs.

Action

Alternate right and left, raising the dumbbells to shoulder height, 1) palm down, 2) rotating palm in, and 3) rotating palm out.

Lower the dumbbells to starting position.

Perform 1 to 3 sets of 3 to 12 reps to tolerance.

5 Standing Barbell Upright Row

MUSCLES TRAINED: Frontal deltoids

Preparation

Stand, with the feet shoulder-width apart or closer.

Position your hands on the barbell nine inches apart, palms facing back.

Action

Pull the barbell until elbows are shoulder height.

Return to the arms-extended position.

Perform 1 to 3 sets of 3 to 12 reps to tolerance.

6 Seated Dumbbell Side-Lateral Raises

MUSCLES TRAINED: Lateral deltoids

Preparation

Sit on the bench, with the feet flat and back straight. Hold dumbbells with palms facing in and arms extended, resting them at your sides.

Action

Keeping elbows in front of shoulders, raise the arms to shoulder height, 1) palms down, 2) palms forward, and 3) palms backward.

Lower the arms to the starting position.

Perform 1 to 3 sets of 3 to 12 reps to tolerance.

1)

7 Seated Rear Lateral Dumbbell Raises

MUSCLES TRAINED: Rear deltoids

Preparation

Sit on the bench, bend forward, feet flat.

Hold dumbbells, palms in and resting on the floor.

Action

Extend your arms out and raise your elbows to shoulder height with palms 1) facing in, 2) facing forward, and 3) facing backward.

Return to the starting position.

Perform 1 to 3 sets of 3 to 12 reps to tolerance.

Upper Back

Chapter 7 includes specific exercises for the upper back. Earlier we delineated the back as two areas, the lower back and upper back, these being two separate muscular regions.

If you recall, we distinguished the lower back as being part of the torso region (lower back and abdominals) of the muscular system. Exercises for the lower back are found in chapter 3, and we hope you will review that chapter. In contrast, the upper back comprises pairs of the latissimus dorsi, trapezius, rhomboids (major and minor), levator scapulae, serratus anterior, and teres major. The upper-back muscles function to produce the movements of adduction and abduction, as well as extension of the shoulder joint. The second group of movements performed by the upper back is elevation, protraction, and retraction of the two scapulas (also see chapter 1).

Let us review the specific functions of the upper back that relate to bodybuilding, sport-specific training, and general fitness training. Bodybuilding, as we have mentioned in previous chapters, attempts to develop the overall size and symmetry of all muscles in the body. For bodybuilders, these same aims guide upper-back training. Bodybuilders are not especially concerned with muscular function in the area, as athletes would be, but rather with the form of muscles.

Athletes, in contrast, are quite concerned with function in the area of the upper back as it applies to their particular sport. Some examples of sport-specific movements encompassing the upper back are throwing a baseball, tackling a football opponent, and serving the ball in tennis. Athletes want to be cross-specific with their training. Analyze the movements performed by the upper back in your sport and then match those movements to exercises performed in the weight room. Always be cross-specific with your training. We do not recommend your aiming to match muscular function for "form" (that is, for bodybuilding) when it comes to athletics.

General fitness enthusiasts look neither to developing massive amounts of muscle nor to hitting home runs in the World Series, so they train their muscles differently. Fitness enthusiasts look more to developing muscular balance in the system and to creating overall strength in the entire body. These same principles hold true with upper-back training among fitness enthusiasts.

Our remarks in chapters 5 and 6 about using machines and free weights and preparing for upper-back work by first doing ROM, flexibility, and stabilization exercises again apply here. Free weights add more difficulty because they recruit synergists during the exercise. Machine weights place the body in a specific position and allow the muscles to move in a specific plane of action. The use of a spotter is always recommended when you use heavy weights or if you are just beginning your training.

1 Wide-Grip Lat Pull-Down to Front

MUSCLES TRAINED: Latissimus

Preparation

Place the feet on the floor, sit, with the hands 24 inches to shoulder width apart.

Extend the arms and lean back slightly.

Action

Pull the bar down toward the upper chest into a Flex-T, and "pinch" the shoulder blades together.

Return to the arms-extended position.

Perform 1 to 3 sets of 3 to 12 reps to tolerance.

2   Single-Arm Dumbbell Row

MUSCLES TRAINED: Latissimus

Preparation

Place one knee and one hand on the bench.

Grasp the dumbbell with the opposite hand, palm straight and arm extended to a resting position on the floor.

Action

With the arm extended, pull the dumbbell up to the side of the chest 1) palm straight, 2) palm in, and 3) palm out.

Extend the arm back to the starting position. Repeat the exercise with the opposite arm.

Perform 1 to 3 sets of 3 to 12 reps in each position to tolerance.

2)

3 Low Cable Pulley Row

MUSCLES TRAINED: Lower latissimus

Preparation

Sit on the bench, back straight, your feet on the platform.

With the knees slightly bent, extend the arms and grasp the handles.

Action

Pull the bar toward the lower abdominals, 1) palms straight, 2) palms in, and 3) palms out.

Return the arms to the extended position; do not lean forward.

Perform 1 to 3 sets of 3 to 12 reps in each position to tolerance.

4 | T-Bar Row

MUSCLES TRAINED: Latissimus

Preparation

Lie on the bench, your feet on the platform.

Extend the arms, with the palms facing back.

Action

Pull your arms toward the chest into a Flex-T and pinch the shoulder blades together, 1) palms back, 2) palms in, and 3) palms out.

Return to the arms-extended position.

Perform 1 to 3 sets of 3 to 12 reps in each position to tolerance.

5 | Close-Grip Front Lat Pull-Downs

MUSCLES TRAINED: Lower latissimus

Preparation

Sit on the bench, your feet flat, with the palms facing in.

Action

Pull the bar to your upper chest.

Return to the arms-extended position.

Do not sway your back during the movement.

Perform 1 to 3 sets of 3 to 12 reps to tolerance.

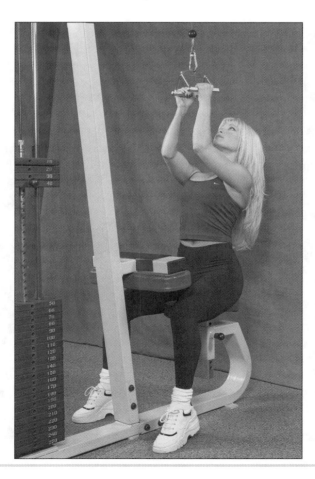

6 Wide-Grip Chin-Ups to the Front

MUSCLES TRAINED: Outer latissimus

Preparation

Extend the arms.

Hold the bar, your palms facing forward, your hands elbow-width apart.

Action

Pull up, eyes level with the bar in a Flex-T.

Return to the arms-extended position. Do not hang with arms straight.

Perform 1 to 3 sets of 3 to 12 reps.

7 Barbell Shrugs

MUSCLES TRAINED: Trapezius

Preparation

Stand, the feet shoulder-width apart or closer.

Hold the bar, arms extended, hands shoulder-width apart.

Action

Raise the shoulders up toward your ears.

Drop the shoulders down to the resting position. Do not let the bar hang with straight arms.

Perform 1 to 3 sets of 3 to 12 reps to tolerance.

8 | Dumbbell Shrugs

MUSCLES TRAINED: Trapezius

Preparation

Stand, the feet shoulder-width apart or closer.

Extend the arms, holding dumbbells with your palms facing inward.

Action

Raise the shoulders up toward your ears.

Drop the shoulders down to the resting position. Do not let the dumbbells hang with straight arms.

Perform 1 to 3 sets of 3 to 12 reps to tolerance.

Biceps and Triceps

Chapter 8 discusses the muscles of the upper arm and sets out exercises for them. The main function of the upper-arm muscles is flexion and extension of the elbow joint. A secondary function of this muscle group is pronation and supination of the arm.

The upper arm is separated into the muscle groupings of the biceps and triceps. The biceps group actually comprises four muscles that flex the arm at the elbow joint: the biceps brachii, brachialis, brachioradialis, and pronator teres. The triceps grouping consists of two muscles: the triceps brachii and anconeus. The triceps brachii is comprised of three heads: lateral, medial, and long. The second muscle in the triceps grouping is the anconeus. This muscle group extends the arm.

We know that any extension or flexion of the arm encompasses these muscles. When we discuss sport specificity, any athletic movement that creates arm action will undoubtedly involve both the triceps and biceps. As is true with other muscles, training those of the upper arm for a specified sport entails matching the specific positions the body is placed in and being *cross-specific*. Cross-specificity is the concept of training the body and its muscles by using the same movements you perform in your sport. When it comes to training the biceps and triceps for a specific sport, therefore, first analyze the movements you use in the sport and perform these same movements in your training.

Swinging a bat is a good example of such cross-specific training for the biceps and triceps. First you would analyze, or break down, the swing to determine its component parts. The second step would be to determine what muscles are involved and what actions they perform in the swing. Then you would use this information to develop the correct training program. In each of the exercises that follow, we list the muscle that is trained: the "biceps" or "outer biceps" describes what area the exercise is working. For example, the standing alternating hammer curl works the lower biceps.

Fitness enthusiasts and bodybuilders want to strive for balance and overall development of the biceps and triceps. Remember, the paramount distinction between a fitness enthusiast and a bodybuilder lies in the overall volumes lifted. In other words, a bodybuilder trains with greater loads and intensity, and the duration of the training is usually longer. Both the fitness enthusiast and bodybuilder should use a variety of exercises in their upper-arm program to allow for training all the functions and muscles of the biceps and triceps muscle groups. The same rules we have discussed for training the chest, upper back, and shoulders with use of machines, free weights, and a spotter apply to training the biceps and triceps, as they do with any other muscle group.

Biceps Exercises

1 | Seated Alternating Dumbbell Curls

MUSCLES TRAINED: Outer biceps

Preparation

Sit on the bench, your feet flat and back straight.

Extend your arms, the palms facing in.

Action

Raise one arm at a time, turning the palm up.

Return the arm to an extended position and raise the opposite arm.

Perform 1 to 3 sets of 3 to 12 reps to tolerance.

2 Standing Biceps Cable Curl

MUSCLES TRAINED: Outer biceps

Preparation

Position your feet shoulder-width apart or narrower.

Extend your arms, with a shoulder-width grip, the palms up.

Action

Curl the bar up to shoulder level.

Return the arms to an extended position.

Perform 1 to 3 sets of 3 to 12 reps to tolerance.

3 Preacher's Bench Barbell Curl

MUSCLES TRAINED: Biceps

Preparation

Sit on the bench, your feet flat, the palms facing up.

Extend the arms, keeping a slight bend in the elbows.

Action

Curl the bar to shoulder height.

Return the arms to the extended position.

Perform 1 to 3 sets of 3 to 12 reps to tolerance.

4 Seated Dumbbell Concentration Curl

MUSCLES TRAINED: Biceps

Preparation

Sit on the bench, holding a dumbbell in one hand.

Rest your elbow on the knee, with your palm facing up.

Action

Curl the dumbbell up to shoulder height.

Return the arm to an extended position.

Perform 1 to 3 sets of 3 to 12 reps to tolerance.

5   Standing Alternating Hammer Curl

MUSCLES TRAINED: Lower biceps

Preparation

Place your feet shoulder-width apart or narrower, with your back straight. Grip dumbbells, your palms facing in.

Action

Curl the right arm up to shoulder height.

Extend the arm to a straightened position.

Repeat with the left arm.

Perform 1 to 3 sets of 3 to 12 reps to tolerance.

6 | Standing Barbell Biceps Curl

MUSCLES TRAINED: Biceps

Preparation
Stand with the feet and hands shoulder-width apart.

Gtip the bar palms up and extend the arms.

Action
Curl the bar to shoulder height.

Return the arms to an extended position.

Perform 1 to 3 sets of 3 to 12 reps to tolerance.

Triceps Exercises

1 Seated Dumbbell Triceps Extension

MUSCLES TRAINED: Triceps

Preparation

Sit on the bench, keeping the back straight. Hold the dumbbell, palms up, in both hands.

Bend the arms to 90°, the dumbbell behind the neck, keeping your palms up.

Action

Extend the arms straight to above the head. Do not lock out the elbows.

Return to the starting position.

Perform 1 to 3 sets of 3 to 12 reps to tolerance.

2 | Triceps Cable Press-Down

MUSCLES TRAINED: Triceps

Preparation

Keep the feet shoulder-width apart, the palms down.

Hold the hands closer than shoulder-width apart (narrow grip).

Bend the elbows, and hold them against your rib cage.

Action

Extend the arms down.

Return to the starting position.

Perform 1 to 3 sets of 3 to 12 reps to tolerance.

3 Seated Barbell Triceps Extension

MUSCLES TRAINED: Triceps

Preparation

Sit on the bench, your feet flat and back straight.

Grip the bar palms up, the hands closer than shoulder-width apart.

Bend the elbows to 90°, and position the bar behind the neck.

Action

Extend the arms to straight above your head. Do not lock out the elbows.

Return to the starting position.

Perform 1 to 3 sets of 3 to 12 reps to tolerance.

4 Flat Bench Barbell Triceps Extension

MUSCLES TRAINED: Triceps

Preparation

Lie on the bench, your feet flat, and grip the bar, palms facing up.

Hands are closer than shoulder-width apart, the arms extended.

Action

Lower the barbell toward your forehead, bending your elbows to 90°.

Extend the arms to the starting position.

Perform 1 to 3 sets of 3 to 12 reps to tolerance.

5 Single-Arm Triceps Cable Extension

MUSCLES TRAINED: Triceps

Preparation

With the feet at shoulder width, square the hips and shoulders toward pulley.

Grip handle, left hand at the right shoulder's level, the palm facing in.

Action

Extend the arm down, rotating the palm outward.

Return to the starting position. Turn around and work other arm.

Perform 1 to 3 sets of 3 to 12 reps to tolerance.

Forearms

Chapter 9 lays out exercises for the forearms, which include 15 muscles. Essentially these forearm muscles can be separated into two categories, the (1) flexion and (2) extension functions involved in moving the wrist. One set of forearm muscles includes the flexors, while the second category includes the extensors.

The forearm flexes and extends not only the wrist but also the hand. These are the two *primary* functions of the forearms, but any grasping movement also involves the forearm muscles. So it goes without saying that most any athletic movement will involve the forearm muscles.

With this group of muscles, as in others that we have discussed, you train in the weight room specifically to the anatomical actions of your sport. In a baseball swing, for instance, flexion and extension of the wrist and hand occur. You would review what wrist actions are involved in the baseball swing and match up the muscular actions of the swing to the appropriate exercises.

Fitness enthusiasts also look to developing wrist strength, hand strength, and muscular balance in their forearm training. Though bodybuilders, in contrast, have these same goals in mind, they also look to increase the size of their forearms. This is done through increased volume, load, and intensity of the forearm workout, which exceed what fitness enthusiasts use.

The exercises in this chapter primarily involve free weights. Very few machines are designed for forearm training. The same principles hold true for the free-weight or machine exercises that pertain to all other exercises. A spotter is again recommended for beginners or for exercisers using heavy loads.

In part 2 of this book we have laid out and described extensive exercises for each anatomical part of the upper body. We have provided a large amount of information on exercises so you can pick and choose what exercises are suitable to form the core portion of your training. To maintain a healthy body and get you to the goals you want to achieve, use this information on core, functional flexibility, and joint-stabilization exercises to develop functional programs specific to your work or play environment.

1 Reverse Grip Barbell Curl

MUSCLES TRAINED: Forearms

Preparation

Place the feet shoulder-width apart or narrower.

Grip bar and hold the hands shoulder-width apart, with the palms facing down.

Extend the arms until barbell rests on thighs.

Action

Curl the arms to shoulder height. Do not change posture with lift.

Return to the starting position.

Perform 1 to 3 sets of 3 to 12 reps to tolerance.

2 **Pronated Barbell Bench Wrist Curl**

MUSCLES TRAINED: Forearms

Preparation

Kneel down, forearms on bench.

Grip bar and hold the hands closer together than shoulder width, with the palms facing down.

Hold the wrists on the edge of the bench, curled downward.

Action

Curl the wrists up.

Return to the starting position.

Perform 1 to 3 sets of 3 to 12 reps to tolerance.

3 Supinated Wrist Curl With Dumbbell

MUSCLES TRAINED: Forearms

Preparation

Kneel down, forearms on bench.

Grip dumbbells and hold the hands shoulder-width apart, with the palms facing upward.

Place the wrists on the edge of the bench, curled down.

Action

Curl the wrists up.

Return to the starting position.

Perform 1 to 3 sets of 3 to 12 reps to tolerance.

4 Supinated Wrist Curl With Barbell

MUSCLES TRAINED: Forearms

Preparation

Kneel down, forearms on bench.

Grip bar and hold the hands shoulder-width apart, with the palms facing upward.

Place the wrists on the edge of the bench, curled down.

Action

Curl the wrists up.

Return to the starting position.

Perform 1 to 3 sets of 3 to 12 reps to tolerance.

PART III
FUNCTIONAL PROGRAMS

In this final portion we combine the foundational principles of muscle strength and the core exercises with machines or free weights into three levels of functional arm and upper body resistance-training programs. Chapter 10 addresses a general conditioning program for total-body fitness and stamina, nutrition/metabolic management, and mental/emotional management. This chapter provides an insurance program of sorts for you. It explains our strongly held view that training the upper body should and can be integrated with conditioning the whole body.

In chapter 11 we explain the differences between training principles applied at the beginning and intermediate levels plus the applications at more advanced levels. Then in chapter 12 we round off these guidelines by showing you how to design your own specific training programs, whether at the beginning, intermediate, or advanced level.

Finally, we give you some practical "to do's," recommendations that we hope will inspire you to strengthen your arms and upper body to reach your personal fitness goals.

CHAPTER 10

General Body Conditioning

Functional fitness involves the *whole* body. In efficient positioning and movement and in balanced strength a sequential muscle loading, from the feet to the fingertips, occurs as energy is absorbed, directed, and delivered in kinetic links. In this chapter we outline total-body fitness and stamina work—in other words, a complete body training to complement the arms and upper-body core training given in part II. We move from the focus on upper body training to looking at the entire body's sound functioning. Arms and shoulders don't move in isolation; they are part of the whole body.

Training for stamina includes aerobic and anaerobic work, and so we identify stamina-building protocols that help the heart and lungs to deliver blood oxygen to muscles, connective tissue, and bone. The second part of the chapter focuses on nutrition and metabolic management of the blood chemistry, endocrine system, and immune system. It tells what's happening inside your body while you train.

Finally, we look at directing mental and emotional energy to enhance your persistence, both personally and professionally. These mental, emotional, motivation "muscles" direct and support your physical efforts as you train for fitness of actual muscles.

Total-Body Fitness Training and Stamina Training

General conditioning is the foundation work for bodybuilding, fitness training, and sport training. It is, first of all, training the body for balanced strength and flexibility to meet the stresses placed on it. General conditioning is functionally integrated, rather than isolated training that works individual muscle groups to create form. Training the body parts to work together is efficient, and integrated training or conditioning works well for both prehabilitation and rehabilitation.

General conditioning benefits from the same philosophy we have emphasized in earlier chapters about the upper body and arms: the body should be trained in a sequence involving (a) position, (b) movement, and (c) resistance in order to develop dynamic balance, trunk stabilization, and joint integrity. Here's an outline of what's involved:

a. Positions (three): straight, supinated, pronated (we'll refer to these as SSP)

b. Movements (three): linear, circular, angular (we'll refer to these as LCA)

c. Resistance protocols (three): integrated flexibility; closed-chain bodywork and stamina work; and open-chain cord and grip, machine and free-weight work.

Integrated Flexibility as a Basic Conditioning Component

Integrated flexibility can be a workout in and of itself. Or it can be a way to elevate the core temperature and warm up to loosen up before a workout sequence. The principles are exactly those we presented in chapter 3, but here they are applied to the whole body, from the feet to the fingertips—a total-body wake-up call! You should do exercises for integrated flexibility three to seven times weekly, using some combination of vertical or standing workouts with horizontal workouts or laying-down workouts.

Standing vertically, start training at the feet and work sequentially up through the various body parts: legs, hips, torso, arms, and hands. Continue up the body to the shoulder area, for which you already know many good flexibility moves. You can find most of these exercises explained and illustrated in chapters 3 and 4; in some instances we add a brief explanation here. Here's a sequence for the shoulders:

1. Shoulder shrugs (LCA), with hands on the hips.
2. Saws, with elbows held stable at 90°.
   a. Move back and forth.
   b. Move the left arm over the right in front.
   c. Move palms up (supinate) and palms down (pronate).
3. Flex-T push-pulls (LCA).
4. Flex-T "Why me?" thumbs up and down.

Bodywork

After integrated flexibility comes bodywork. Bodywork should be done three to four times a week using the total body—feet to fingertips—to your level of time and tolerance. (You've seen a lot of this in chapter 2, but a quick review won't hurt.)

Push-ups. Here are two variations for your bodywork push-ups:

1. With a Flex-T at the shoulders and using the three hand positions (SSP).
2. With one arm in a Flex-T at the shoulders and the other arm doing one-arm push-ups.

Seated butt-ups. Do seated butt-ups with a shoulder pinch, holding the hands just under your hips in four hand positions (SSP plus straight backward).

Elbow-ups. Add a couple of versions of the elbow-ups, both from a prone position.

1. Lie belly down in a Dead Frog (for the feet)–cobra position (for the upper body); using or going through the forearms in three positions (SSP), pinch the shoulder blades together three to five times in each forearm position.
2. Lie flat out, belly up; start with the hands on your thighs, then move them to the belly button area as a variation; then place your thumbs in your armpits as a third variation; and finally, place the hands behind the head. In each hand position, keep the elbows on the ground, lift the head and shoulders, and pinch the shoulder blades together.

Side-ups. Position—move to your side, and line up the ankles, knees, hips, and spine, with the elbow and forearm at 90° on the ground. Your off arm should be in a Flex-T, and the hand placed on the hip. Then do these variations:

1. Move the body straight up and down.
2. While the head stays stable, the body does a quarter turn and moves straight up and down.
3. The entire body rotates on its axis of forearm and feet toward the ground (that is, the hip turns), and then performs the side-ups and -downs.

Trunk moves. Position yourself with or without a plyoball between the knees; hold your knees up, keeping the back flat, the knees at 90°, and the thumbs in your armpits in a Flex-T. Then do these variations:

1. Knees to the nose, then to the right and left shoulders.
2. With a back flat, the knees at 90°, and the hands behind the head or next to the hips, do a nose (a) to the knees, (b) to the right and left shoulders, (c) to the right and left knees, and then (d) knee extensions.
3. With the back flat, knees at 90°, and a plyoball in the hands, do trunk twists and then right and left tick-tocks with the arms extended.

Leg stabilizers. To work for balance and stability with the legs, lean against the wall vertically ("air benches"), with the knees at 90°, back flat against wall, and thumbs in the armpits. Keep the toes first straight, then supinated, and then pronated. Hold 30 to 120 seconds in each position to tolerance.

Cord and Grip Work

By definition this type of workout requires elastic cords of different tensile strengths and having an ergonomically correct grip. The training protocol is designed to enhance joint stability and endurance, and it integrates the synergists and movements specific to your work or play. Do the cord and grip work between three and seven times per week.

Cord and body. Proceed the same as with vertical integrated flexibility workouts, working upward, from the lower body to the abs and lower back and then up to shoulder shrugs. Depending on how far the cord is stretched, you can increase or decrease resistance depending on your tolerance. Refer back to the chapters on flexibility and bodywork (see chapters 3 and 4 especially). Add these workouts, too:

1. Biceps, triceps curls.
2. Flys.

Cord, body, and a prop. Anchor your elastic cord to a pole or post, a door, or a fence. These are some effective variations to use, doing between 5 and 15 reps:

1. Flex-T shoulder-blade scapular pinches, your hands alternating between SSP positions.
2. Flex-T circles forward and backward, SSP hand position.
3. Flex-T swims forward and backward, SSP hand position.
4. Flex-T hitchhikers; thumbs up, thumbs down, right and left, one arm at a time.
5. Two-arm Flex-Ts, thumbs up to thumbs down.
6. Reverse Flex-T, same as 1, 2, and 3.
7. Two-arm reverse Flex-T, thumbs down to thumbs up.

Stamina Work

Once you have this total-body training protocol in place, you can properly implement stamina work. It involves aerobic and anaerobic preparations, and you should include it in your workouts between three and seven times per week.

Stamina, loosely defined, is cardiopulmonary efficiency. Think of it this way. Your heart and lungs form the delivery system for blood . . . the fuel source for all your physical activity. Blood provides oxygen and nutrients to muscles, connective tissue, and bones for preparing and repairing the body in your work or play environment. In micro- and macrocycles, stamina is all about oxygen—developing the aerobic and anaerobic capacity of your cardiopulmonary system. Basically, *aerobic* means there is oxygen available; *anaerobic* means there's a high-use level or lack of oxygen. And the more oxygen the muscles get, the longer they can work, the faster they can recover, and the *stronger* they can get. Stamina work is aerobic and anaerobic preparation.

Aerobic Preparation

In aerobic preparation you are teaching your body to utilize oxygen efficiently. It is a constant flow of oxygen into your lungs, which can be delivered to your muscles by your heart at a uniform, comfortable rate. Walking, jogging, regular or stationary cycling, swimming—any of these activities will work. Low impact–no impact is easier on the joints because aerobic work does require 20 to 40 minutes of activity three to seven times per week.

At this point we could talk about intensity levels and training zones for aerobic efficiency but it isn't necessary. There's a simple benchmark for appropriate aerobic work: if you can't carry on a conversation during aerobic activity, your intensity level is too high.

You are after oxygen, not effort. Here's something that will help you gain a perspective. There are only 15 calories' (of effort) difference in an hour's worth of brisk walking versus an hour's worth of jogging!

If you walk or jog—outside, inside, on a treadmill, or in the shallow end of a pool—try going backward and sideways (kariokes), to tolerance, for a portion of your workout. If you are outside, make sure to pick a flat, safe surface. Treadmills are ideal because they have rails for balance. If you ride a stationary bike, pedal backward for a portion of your ride. Why forward, backward, and sideways? The combination recruits all the movement muscles of your extremities and forces the abs and low-back muscles to work extra to stabilize your torso and posture. The same concept of combinations works as well for sit-ups and crunches! Give it a try, you'll be surprised.

Is weight management one of your workout goals? Aerobic work (with proper nutrition) burns fat best. Finally, if you can, mix in pool work to overcome both mental stress and the physical stresses of neural stagnation and monotonous overtraining. Work in a pool also gives joints a break from the impact of running and weight lifting.

Anaerobic Preparation

When you talk exercise intensity and lung capacity, or training to increase $\dot{V}O_2$max, you really mean anaerobic preparation. The amount of oxygen your lungs can accommodate is a function of the lungs' size and efficiency. Training your lungs to get bigger and better at delivering oxygen in the blood stream means putting your total body into oxygen debt, using short bursts of intense physical activity, short recovery time, and a lot of frequency.

Sprint work on the ground or in the water, hill work, plyometric work, stepping, leaping, and bounding are good outdoor activities. Jumping rope is an effective anaerobic training activity for indoors. Mix and match here, and your $\dot{V}O_2$max will increase accordingly.

One last thought about building your stamina. Fitness inside the body is just as important for big, muscled bodybuilders as it is for lean-and-mean body shapers. It facilitates muscles, both their preparing and repairing, and enhances the overall quality of life between micro- and macro-training cycles.

OK, now that you know about how to build a better supply of blood oxygen, let's discuss developing better blood chemistry through nutrition and metabolic management.

Nutrition and Metabolic Management

A functional metabolism to support your work or play environment requires nutritional conditioning—creating a balance between the physical activity you desire and the blood chemistry needed to support it. This is accomplished by combining, rotating, supplementing, and enhancing foods.

If you think of this balance as metabolic management, it may help you dispel some misinformation about fitness and fatness. Your body's metabolism is an engine that's always "on," whether it's on idle (while you're sleeping) or on red line (when you're working out or competing). If you tune your body properly with training and fuel it properly with nutrition, it's going to be more efficient. Paradoxically, muscle and blood chemistry (through homeostasis) tend to help each other, with or without your assistance, but at a price.

We North Americans are obsessed with fat, probably because no matter what we try, we're still getting fatter. This obsession doesn't help you get your upper body to look the way you want it to, and it actually threatens the quality of your life. A myriad of health-related issues attend to being either overweight or "underfatted."

Yes, we said *under*fatted! Believe it or not, your body needs fat. Depending on your genetics and metabolic requirements, "smart fat" should constitute 10 to 33 percent of your daily nutritional intake. Of course, this is blasphemy in our low-fat or no-fat world, but fat is actually the symptom, not the illness. A slender, nonfit female on a low-fat or no-fat, high-carbohydrate diet may be more "at risk" for difficulties with her metabolism than is a slightly overweight, in-shape middle-aged male!

So if fat's not where it's at, what is? It's *fitness*, not *fatness*. Start paying attention to your shape while you're getting in shape. Stored fat burns last; so measure your inches, not your pounds. Body density (see table 10.1) is a more important measurement and fitness indicator than is body fat because lean muscle weighs more than fatty muscle. Nerves work in the muscles—they don't work in fat—and it takes four times more energy to move a pound of fat than it does a pound of muscle. In effect, you can dine—not diet—be heavier with a smaller waistline, have more energy, and move more efficiently at work or play if you get *fit with function*. And this takes us right back to proper training for stronger arms and a better upper body.

When health officials recently redefined fitness in 1998, some 29 million Americans turned overweight "overnight." Here is a portion of a chart, showing new standards of height, body-mass index (BMI), and weight:

Table 10.1

STANDARDS OF HEIGHT, BODY-MASS INDEX (BMI), AND WEIGHT

$$\text{Body-Mass Index (BMI)} = \frac{703 \times \text{weight in pounds}}{(\text{height in inches})^2}$$

	Healthy	Previously healthy, now overweight			Overweight	
BMI →	**23**	**24**	**25**	**26**	**27**	**28**
5'	118	123	128	133	138	143
5'1"	122	127	132	137	143	148
5'3"	130	135	141	146	152	158
5'5"	138	144	150	156	162	168
5'7"	146	153	159	166	172	178
5'9"	155	162	169	176	182	189
5'11"	165	172	179	186	193	200
6'1"	174	182	189	197	204	212
6'3"	184	192	200	208	216	224

Source: *Newsweek* (July 1998).

Balancing Activity and Blood Chemistry

Food *combining* means finding the proper ratio of protein, complex and simple carbohydrates, and smart fat. Food *rotating* involves trying not to eat the same food prepared the same way twice within a 72-hour period. Food *supplementing* refers to finding the proper combination of vitamins, minerals, digestive enzymes, and anti-oxidants to help your body overcome whatever shortcomings might exist in your daily diet (see table 10.2 for a list of dietary supplements).

Preservatives, growth hormones, overcooking, and overprocessing make foods dangerously interactive with so-called free radicals and carcinogenics in the body. Supplements, in general, help your blood and immune system to do battle with this "bad stuff."

Scientists have long linked green tea to the low rates of stomach cancer and heart disease found in some Asian populations. And new findings suggest that black tea, which comes from the same leaves, offers similar benefits. Tea leaves are richer than most fruits and vegetables in antioxidant compounds called flavonoids and polyphenols. These chemicals seem to inhibit tumor growth and may also combat arterial blockages that lead to heart attacks or strokes.

Principles of Food Enhancement

Food *enhancing* refers to finding the proper combination of metabolic boosters or potentiators to complement (1) genetics and (2) physical training for improved work or play performance. Think of enhancements this way: they don't make you bigger, faster, or stronger by themselves, but they do allow you to work harder and recover quicker, which, in turn, optimizes genetic potential and physical preparation time. Because there is so much misinformation in the media about this process, it's important to set down some basic assumptions, principles, and applications here.

Let's first look at some commonly accepted assumptions. We have consulted with several dedicated people[1] in addition to

[1] We consulted Rick Heitsch, MD (at the Northwest Center for Environmental Health, 503-261-0966); James Bradshaw (at Southern California Sports Supplements, 619-456-5686); Maggie Zepf (at the Great Earth Vitamin Store, 619-481-5583); and Tyler Seltzer (at Seltzer Chemicals, 760-438-0089).

Table 10.2

SUPPLEMENTS

Digestive enzymes (help metabolize protein, carbohydrates, and fats)

Megavitamins (help if you are short of the necessary vitamins in your regular diet)

Megaminerals (help if you are short of the necessary minerals)

Vitamin C (antioxidant; aids collagen tissue)

Vitamin E (antioxidant; cardiovascular aid and HDL booster)

Beta-carotene (antioxidant; helps lung and eye tissue, fights ultraviolet light)

Selenium (antioxidant; fights cancer, helps liver)

Pycnogynol (antioxidant; helps connective tissue, joints, nerves)

Lycopene (antioxidant, cancer fighter)

Alpha lipoic acid (antioxidant, promotes glucose uptake, endurance, cell protection)

CoQ10 (antioxidant, helps mitochondria [heart muscle], boosts ATP)

Folic acid (helps heart functions, tissue recovery)

Branched chain amino acids (help the body as a lean-muscle facilitator along with exercise)

Chromium picolinate (helps as a fat burner with exercise)

Glucosamine sulfate (helps facilitate healthy joints and connective tissue)

Acidophilus (helps facilitate digestion, boosts natural bacteria in the digestive tract)

Gingko biloba (facilitates blood circulation, helps memory)

Kava (may help overcome mild anxiety)

St.-John's-wort (helps overcome mild depression)

Echinacea (helps ward off colds and flu as an immune-system booster) reading research reports. First, we agree with the Barry Sears *Zone Diet* as a good starting point: that is, 40 percent carbohydrates, 30 percent fats, and 30 percent protein in the daily diet. Refinement of these percentages is necessary on an individual basis, of course, for optimal performance. This refinement is a function of personal history and what genetic information is available. As genetic research evolves, this information should be continuously updated, and you then must adjust your diet accordingly.

Second, performance is limited to genetic potential: it is a function of metabolic typing, glycolipids, and essential sugar uptake by the body during physical activity. These sugars are basically polysaccharides and monosaccharides, which are recognition molecules to help the immune system.

Genetic potential complements our previously mentioned four areas of sport performance: efficiency of mechanics, psychological conditioning, physical conditioning for strength, and nutritional conditioning for energy production. Although the genetics related to energy production in the body is similar in the basics among all mammals and even more so among all humans, there is sufficient variability in the details to make it complex and difficult to achieve the true genetic potential in any individual.

Getting an adequate supply of necessary nutrients is imperative for optimal physiology. These include energy sources (calories), water, oxygen, cofactors (vitamins and minerals), and specific nutrients the body needs and cannot otherwise produce (essential fatty acids, essential amino acids, and maybe certain essential sugars and other carbohydrates). We still have much to learn, certainly about essential sugars and other carbohydrates.

It seems clear, however, that the human body has the genetic potential to respond to circumstances as necessary if it receives the necessary raw materials. It can also recognize the need for, and produce, those chemicals necessary to deal with the situation. As an example, a meal high in carbohydrates causes the release (and remanufacture) of hormones, insulin, cortisone, and thyroid hormone, which causes the liver to make and release lipogenic enzymes. These in turn cause the carbohydrates to be converted to and stored as fat. This sequence does not occur unless the body meets up with the need—the high carbohydrate meal.

However, please be aware that the genetic potential of the individual determines his or her capacity to regulate these materials of any system. In people with limited or exceeded capacity to handle carbohydrates, for example, insulin insensitivity develops, triggering type II diabetes.

Pattern of Task-Related Energy

Task-related energy follows a certain pattern. Rest periods are linked to the energy source being utilized for the goals being achieved. The body uses three different energy systems for specific exercise regimens (see figure 10.1). For high-intensity exercise that lasts fewer than 30 seconds, the primary energy sources are adenosine triphosphate (ATP) and creatine phosphate. Exercise of moderate intensity lasting between 30 seconds and two minutes utilizes the faster glycolytic system, and exercises of low intensity lasting longer than two minutes use the body's oxidative system for fuel.

This energy pattern becomes important in determining the potential sport-related or training-related effects of diet and dietary supplements. What supplements to take, in other words, depends in part on which ones enhance energy production and stamina, and therefore encourage an increase in performance.

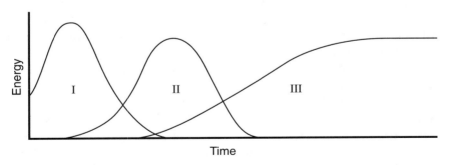

I. From 0-6 seconds, uses ATP and glycogen stored in muscle; explosive high force and very brief activity.

II. From 10 seconds to several minutes, uses various energy sources; anaerobic, exceeds oxygen supply, and is limited by the accumulation of lactic acid.

III. From 15 minutes to several hours, uses glucose and fat and finally protein for energy; aerobic, warm up slowly to activate enzymes, and the ability to up-regulate enzymes is determined by conditioning plus genetics, which determines stamina.

Figure 10.1 Energy-time graph of the three fuel systems.

Blood-Chemistry Boosters

Dietary enhancements, or potentiators, can be divided into two categories: blood-chemistry boosters and hormone boosters. With this in mind, are there performance-enhancing diets and dietary supplements? Yes.

Creatine Monohydrate

Creatine is an essential nutrient composed of amino acids. It is produced naturally by the body for the purposes of supplying energy for muscular contractions. Manufacturers claim that supplements can yield increases in muscle size and strength when they are combined with resistance exercises, such as weight lifting. Creatine increases the supply of phosphates used in adenosine triphosphate (ATP) production. This means that when ATP is used in an activity (and converted to ADP with energy release), the restoration to ATP may be faster and more consistent. The net effect is that for explosive actions, those using ATP, an athlete recovers faster and longer. Translated into practical terms, for example, in throwing a baseball you should be able to maintain velocity for more throws.

Increased weight and muscle girth probably are the result of fluid retention in the muscle; fluid retention in other tissues is a recognized side effect. Here's the bottom line: creatine monohydrate is probably of some value, but its usefulness is limited by side effects as well as by an individual's genetic potential (it doesn't work at all, for example, in 20 to 30 percent of people.) It has not improved sprint performance in running or swimming.

Several respected studies, including one in the *European Journal of Applied Physiology* and another in the journal *Clinical Science,* have established that 20 to 30 grams a day of creatine monohydrate improved strength related to high-intensity anaerobic exercises (such as weightlifting and short-burst, sprint-level cycling). The supplement also appeared to delay the onset of muscular exhaustion during high-intensity anaerobic workouts. However, these and other studies have noted that athletes who engage in endurance sports—such as running, long-distance cycling, and other aerobic activities—are not likely to benefit, because the energy systems they primarily use rely more on oxygen than on creatine.

Is creatine monohydrate safe? There have been no reports of significant adverse effects, although some medical journals have published anecdotal letters from physicians citing an increased incidence of muscle cramping and dehydration among patients who take creatine. Again, however, no long-term studies of the product's safety have yet been conducted.

Beta-Hydroxy-Beta-Methylbutyrate (HMB)

Beta-Hydroxy-Beta-Methylbutyrate (HMB) is a by-product of the natural amino acid leucine. Because, the theory goes, leucine regulates protein metabolism, high amounts of HMB can reduce the breakdown of proteins and thereby lead to increased muscle strength and size. Two credible studies, one of them published in the *Journal of Applied Physiology,* indicate that HMB does indeed work. Both studies had subjects take three grams of HMB daily while embarking on an exercise program; the subjects' increases in muscle mass and strength and their decreases in body fat were significantly greater than those experienced by control-group subjects, who did not take the supplement.

No side effects have been reported, but no safety tests have yet been performed.

Ephedrine

An alkaloid derived from the ephedra plant, ephedrine is included in a variety of products that tout increased energy and weight loss. Both advocates and detractors acknowledge that ephedrine, an amphetamine, stimulates the central nervous and cardiovascular systems. Some people interpret the resulting effects as increased energy; others describe them as nervousness, hyperactivity, or mania.

Between January 1993 and May 1998 the FDA logged more than 800 complaints of adverse events associated with people who had taken ephedrine, including instances of seizures, breathing difficulties, vomiting, palpitations, and even the deaths of some 40 people (among them some who were young, active men). Of particular concern, investigators note, are products that combine ephedrine with caffeine, which may enhance ephedrine's effects. The FDA is now seeking to restrict recommended dosages of ephedrine. Manufacturers say that not enough is known about the reported cases of death and illness associated with ephedrine to conclude that the substance was to blame. They insist that ephedrine is safe if used as directed. Again, no definitive research has been done.

Pyruvate

Mechanisms of improved stamina and glucose usage seem to be based on pyruvate's effect as a stimulus that up-regulates various enzyme systems in the presence of certain endogenous hormones. Early studies were performed to evaluate carbohydrate loading in untrained subjects, and pyruvate does stimulate this effect. Value appears to decrease as the training level of the athlete increases, and recent studies indicate that pyruvate may have long-term effects similar to a high carbohydrate diet (insulin tolerance, etc.). Here's the bottom line: pyruvate may be useful in the same sense that carbohydrate loading is, but the value is much less in well-conditioned athletes; it may stimulate stamina but not explosive activity.

Gamma Oryzanol

Gamma oryzanol and its main active ingredient, ferulic acid, appear to increase the muscle cells' ability to extract glucose from blood. Several years of active research and attempts to develop a useful product have not resulted in much use up to now, and the data are still coming in. If gamma oryzanol proves useful, it will probably be for stamina rather than for any enhancement of explosive movement.

Hormone Boosters

Interest in the use of hormone boosters has grown in the recent decades among athletes who seek to enhance their performances. These supplements, however, have also raised equal amounts of concern.

Human Growth Hormone

Resistance training, at any age, will initiate the release of growth hormone into the blood and body chemistry. Taken externally, human growth hormone (HGH) can be used as an anti-aging agent. It can improve muscle tone and enhance an overall sense of well-being. In moderate doses (up to four international units per week), no side effects or only minimal ones occur, but the hormone's real value for *young* athletes is questionable. There are many supplements that enhance the natural release of HGH into the blood. For mature adults, these formulas are probably an effective, safe, and inexpensive way of achieving more return for time and training effort.

Androstenedione

"Andro" or androstenedione is a direct hormone precursor, used by the body to create testosterone, the primary compound for regulating the growth and repair of muscle tissue. Companies that market andro assert that if you increase your body's supply (via supplementation) of this building block of testosterone, you will raise your testosterone levels and thus gain muscle mass and physical strength.

The statistics on andro's effectiveness that manufacturers cite most often come from a 20-year-old East German study, however, that was performed as part of a patent application. That document asserted that 100 milligrams of andro taken daily were capable of boosting testosterone levels by as much as 237 percent in men and 600 percent in women. Advertisements for andro often fail to note the different rates of effect in men and women, and simply claim increases of 237 to 600 percent. But the East Germans used a form of the substance that was administered nasally, purported to be more readily absorbed than the oral form used in the United States. As of this writing, no U.S.–based studies have been published about the effects that andro supplementation has on testosterone production, although new research was recently conducted at the University of Texas at Arlington and some information about it was released in February 1999.

No safety studies have been conducted. Critics theorize that artificially elevating testosterone levels could cause problems, ranging from an increased chance of heart attacks to serious psychological conditions. Advocates counter that the testosterone increases are comparatively small and unlikely to cause significant side effects. Both sides agree that teenage boys, who already have high levels of testosterone due to puberty, should *not* use andro or other steroid hormones.

DHEA (Dehydroepiandrosterone)

Like androstenedione, DHEA (dehydroepiandrosterone) stimulates the body to create testosterone. Those who advocate using DHEA suggest that it can increase muscle mass, inhibit aging, and improve one's mental well-being.

The oft-quoted studies, one in the *Journal of Clinical Endocrinology and Metabolism* and the other in *Annals of the New York Academy of Sciences*, observed testosterone-level increases in men over 40 years old who took DHEA. It's not clear whether this effect directly correlates with any "anti-aging" claims, such as decreased fat composition. It's also unclear whether men under 40 years of age would benefit in any way from the compound. The notion of testosterone depletion as a primary factor still is under investigation.

Critics say that because the compound is a precursor not just to testosterone but also to estrogen, it can cause breast enlargement in men. They also say it may increase the risk of prostate cancer. Proponents maintain that short-term use at low levels (no more than 50 milligrams a day) is safe. In 1996 the FDA technically banned DHEA for sale as a therapeutic substance used to combat aging, lowered libido, and other conditions. But manufacturers continue to sell it as a dietary supplement, invoking the 1994 protective legislation.

Other Hormone Boosters

Various other hormone boosters are available and occasion interest. Here's a quick outline of them:

- Diascorhea is a precursor to other steroid hormones, and its conversion to useful forms varies.
- Pregnenolone is still closer to other steroid hormones and a step down the desired conversion pathway, so its usefulness is questionable.
- Anabolic steroids have some effects, such as increased muscle mass and aggressiveness, that are well known, but so are the complications connected with the heart and circulatory system, as well as with cancer.

Bottom line? Until more is known about long-term side effects, be smart, be conservative, and do not experiment without supervision with *any* of the hormone enhancers.

At this time we would not suggest any more than physiological (vs. pharmacological) doses of DHEA (<50 mg/day), pregnenolone (<100 mg/day), or androstenedione (<100 mg/day). We do *not* recommend anabolic steroids because proven or potential side effects outweigh their possible benefits.

Remember, it's the training that returns the reward, *not* the chemical. Use your head! And that admonition is a perfect segue into the final section of this chapter on overall body conditioning.

Mental and Emotional Management

We all know that without the proper mind-set your physical preparation, nutritional preparation, and biomechanical preparation are marginal at best. But how does an individual find and keep a proper mind-set? How does an individual stay motivated to train, given all the stresses, distresses, and distractions of daily living? While there are no easy answers, we have found that some factors are common among both motivated elite athletes and everyday individuals.

The number-one factor is persistence. Motivated people find a way to get their training done. Persistence is personal—a decision to improve quality of life, a change in paradigms created by commitment, consistency, and convenience. These "three C's" are vital for adequate preparation. All forms of preparation must be accomplished with some semblance of *self-direction*.

Self-direction can tip the scales in favor of or against you. Unless you're self-directed, though you may survive, you won't thrive. Self-direction is a glue that holds it all together for you. If you observe successful people, you'll find that every one of them—no matter what economic background, intelligence, age, or race the individual brings along—goes through certain processes that lead to being self-directed.

First, you must know yourself in order to help yourself. There are four distinguishable levels of self-awareness you must go through, which function somewhat based on levels of talent or skill, information or experience, and performance at work or play:

1. Unconsciously incompetent (you know "nothing" and can't do anything)
2. Consciously incompetent (you know something, but you can't do anything with that knowledge)
3. Unconsciously competent (you have little if any awareness, but you do it anyway)
4. Consciously competent (you know what you need to know and are successful in doing it)

Obviously, you'd like to be at level four eventually. The third level works until someone starts failing too often and doesn't know how to fix the failure. The second level is usually a problem of talent or skill that results in a less-than-rewarding quality of life, and the first category is just "entry" level.

To have self-awareness requires objective self-assessment. Look at these four levels as a way to determine where you are currently, even if where you are isn't where you want to be. Then you can define where you want to be and "connect the dots" to get there. This exercise helps focus the mind and body to make your preparation a lot more efficient.

By defining a goal or a series of objectives, you don't end up working hard and going nowhere. Of course, assessing where you are is sometimes upsetting—a wake-up call to reality. Don't let this impede your path to self-improvement or self-direction.

Understanding self-emotion is a prerequisite to being self-directed. You learn to manage optimal levels of emotion—not to control them, but to direct them. Anger, elation, aggression, fear, anxiety, and insecurity all are normal emotions. They are even acceptable in the work or playing environment if they're vented appropriately—at the right time and place and for appropriate reasons. In sport and life, successful veterans experience these intense emotions in competition, the same as do hotheaded rookies. The difference is that the veterans have learned to manage them properly. They seldom let emotion get in the way of competition, for instance. Managing your emotions is a learned skill, and it can become an important coping tool for success—and failure.

Most people understand about being objective, and view feedback about success or failure at work as a valid external benchmark. It's the *feeling* that goes with the success or failure, however, that often causes problems. That feeling is internal and unique to the individual. You process the feeling psychologically, neurologically, immunologically and it causes a fight-flee-or-freeze response in your body! Emotions are subsets of these physiological responses. The feelings and emotions are normal, and they can occur at any time with anyone and in any combination. Embrace the feelings, work them, manage them. Just don't let them impede your preparation or long-term performance.

Managing your motivation is another important part of being self-directed. Fitness is an arena for failure as well as success. Anyone can stay motivated when things go well. But you must be aware going in that, because of the natural inevitability of some failures, staying motivated will require persistence on your part. Figure out quickly what keeps you motivated, because only the persistent thrive.

Here are some affirmations we have found helpful:

- Before every important decision, I ask myself, What ought to be done for me? Will it injure others or me? Is it in accord with my beliefs and goals? Is it aligned with reality as I see it? Am I willing to fully accept the consequences?
- To be truly successful in my pursuit and to grow in self-esteem, I persist in my growth, pursuit of fulfillment, or happiness.

- I choose to treat myself with dignity and proceed to move toward success with passion, wisdom, freedom, and joy. I am the authority over me.

- To release my competitive potential from past restrictive programming of my subconscious, I give myself the right to be me and to function as I choose. I cannot have sound self-esteem if I am not true to myself or if I give up responsibility and accountability for my own life as I seek to achieve my goals.

- I want to allow myself the freedom to choose success without building a prison of "have to," "can't," and "they won't let me."

- I function from my own free choice. I can recognize myself as an important, valuable, and interesting person or as an absolute incompetent who is unworthy and unneeded. I can choose to be kind, caring, helpful, loyal, and compassionate or to be lazy, cowardly, mean, and disloyal. I choose to be happy, free, and successful.

- By allowing myself this freedom, I recognize that I am responsible for my decisions and actions, and I am willing to accept the consequences they bring.

- I know I am the one who will answer for my action and will profit or suffer accordingly.

- Someone else's opinion of me has nothing to do with what I think of myself.

Proper preparation, good information, and instruction make the whole process efficient and effective. Ultimately, it's the synergy of persistence with proper preparation that keeps you motivated, gets you out of the box, and improves your quality of life.

The law of inertia applies to the pursuit of fitness or improved functioning: an object at rest wants to remain at rest. To *overcome your personal inertia,* remember the old adage that every long journey is begun with one short step. Your personal best—in attaining fitness—is a journey that requires just one step at a time. Bodybuilders don't get big overnight; they get big over time. Marathoners don't run 26 miles the first day they train. People don't get fat and out of shape overnight; it, too, happens over time. Take that first step and the next step will be easier. Continue the steps one at a time and, over time, you reach your goal!

CHAPTER 11

Principles of Advanced Training

We have already provided a complete outline of flexibility, joint-stabilization, and core resistance-training exercises in chapters 3 through 9. Before laying out specific exercise programs in chapter 12, we introduce you here to the terminology and principles of more advanced training.

Types of Advanced Training

Exercises can be classified by type. We describe and use three classification systems to help you in setting up a program and evaluating it. The first classification system divides exercises according to their load and force curve. The second system divides exercises into two categories based on the joints involved in performing them: multijoint and single-joint exercises. The third classification system separates exercises in terms of the movement plane in which they are done.

System 1: Isotonic, Isometric, and Isokinetic Exercises

Training comprises three broad types of exercises. Many programs implement only one category, while others use all three to benefit the individual. These three categories of exercise, which depend on loads and force curves, are isotonic, isometric, and isokinetic.

Isotonic exercises encompass a load that remains constant, but the resistance acting on the muscles varies with the joint's angle. An example is free-weight training. A biceps curl exercise has a constant weight throughout the movement, but the resistance varies in terms of the angle at the elbow joint; that is, the resistance changes as the angle changes. The common movements of muscle fibers in isotonic exercises are called *concentric* and *eccentric*. Concentric muscle action is a shortening of the muscle fibers during contraction. Eccentric muscle action is a lengthening of the muscle as it develops tension. Using the biceps curl as an example, the concentric action occurs as you raise the barbell, whereas the eccentric action occurs as you lower the barbell.

Isometric exercise occurs when a static contraction of the muscle results. The contraction of muscle is performed against a fixed object, and the muscle does not shorten or lengthen during the exercise.

Isokinetic exercise, in contrast, uses exercises where accommodating resistance exists. The action of constant load through a ROM (range of motion) is defined as accommodating resistance. So isokinetic exercises include both ecccentric and concentric actions and occur when the load remains constant through the force curve developed in the muscle action. Implemented by specific machines, isokinetic exercises are often used for rehabilitation.

System 2: Multijoint and Single-Joint Exercises

In this classification system, we split exercises not by force curves and loads, but rather by the movement of the exercise itself. Most of the exercises we have described can be sorted into either single-joint or multijoint exercises. The classification process with single-joint and multijoint exercises closely depends on the human body's physiology.

Multijoint exercises are based on the principle of skeletal joint movement. A multijoint exercise involves moving more than one joint through a specified range of motion. The bench press is a good example of a multijoint exercise: both the elbow joint and the shoulder joint are involved in the movement.

An exercise is classified as a single-joint exercise when only one skeletal joint is moved through a range of motion during the action. The barbell curl is a ready example of a single-joint exercise: the bar is lifted through a range of motion involving only the elbow joint.

System 3: Movement Planes and Exercises

Another way to train is by using exercise in different body planes (see figure 11.1). Anatomists divide the body into three movement planes:

sagittal, transverse, and frontal. The *sagittal plane* divides the body on a longitudinal line, in other words, into a left and right side. A biomechanical movement occurring in this plane would be categorized as being in the "sagittal" plane. For example, in a biceps barbell curl, the elbow joint is flexed and extended in the sagittal plane.

The *transverse plane* divides the body anatomically into upper and lower halves or divisions. The transverse plane is perpendicular to the sagittal plane. An easy way to remember this movement plane is to envision a circular plane essentially drawn around the midsection

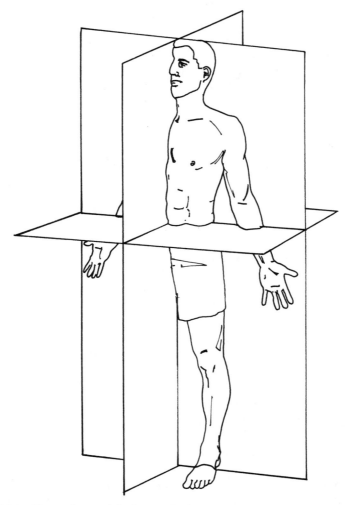

Figure 11.1 Three planes of the human body.

of the body, dividing the body at the torso into a top and lower half. A biomechanical movement in the transverse movement plane is *rotational* in terms of a joint. For instance, internal rotation of the shoulder occurs in the transverse plane. Left and right rotation of the neck occurs in the transverse plane.

The *frontal plane* divides the body into a front and back. The flexion and extension of the trunk to the left and right is an example of a biomechanical movement in this plane.

The point to note is that biomechanical movements occur in many planes. The body is not one-dimensional in terms of movement; it functions in three dimensions. We've emphasized throughout the book that human movement is by turns linear, circular, and angular. If the body moves in different planes, then the muscles used to move extremities and surrounding joints should be trained to reflect this movement order. To be functional, whether in basic or in advanced resistance training, you need a proper protocol involving the prime movers, secondary movers, and synergistic movers *in all three movement planes.*

Training Guidelines

You now have substantial information to help you begin setting up your training program. In this section we add some guidelines and a review of some important principles to help you out.

Start With the Core Exercises

The first point to remember is this: begin your program with the core exercises. A secondary exercise can fatigue a specific part of the muscle or muscle group; as a result of this fatigue, you would derive less benefit from your core exercises if they came afterward. This is a rule of thumb for developing your program. A few advanced techniques might alter or supersede this principle, but overall keep this as a general focus point.

Place core exercises at the beginning of your program, and institute secondary exercises afterward.

Train Large to Small or Small to Large?

Think back to the upper body's six muscle groups. If you are after *hypertrophy* or *power,* you should train larger muscle groups first and sequence downward to the smaller muscle groups and synergists. The reason is that, as you perform exercises for the larger muscle groups of the upper body, many of the smaller muscles will function to assist the primary movers. For example, during the barbell bench press, the pectoral muscle is the primary mover of the lift, but the shoulder and triceps muscles assist in the movement. Doing exercises for the triceps prior to doing chest exercises causes the pectorals to suffer—because an assistant muscle has been prefatigued.

On the other hand, if you are working for flexibility, endurance, balance (or all three) and not size, then you should work from small to large—synergist to prime mover. This protocol fatigues muscles uniformly, leading to hypertrophic parity, or muscle balance.

Train With Multijoint Before Single-Joint Exercises

In the second classification of exercises, recall that multijoint exercises have movements using more than one joint while going through a specified range of motion, whereas single-joint exercises take only a single joint through a certain range of motion. You want to do exercises that involve multiple joints before those that use only a single joint. Add this idea to the training of core and secondary, large, medium, and small muscle groups, and match it up with your needs and goals.

To integrate multijoint and single-joint exercises into your program, start with a multijoint exercise, which will recruit large muscle groups or the use of more than one muscle group to perform the exercise. Then, in prioritizing exercise order, choose an exercise making lower demands on muscle recruitment *after* the multijoint work.

Let's summarize:

- For size and power
    a. use solid resistance-training programs,
    b. train larger muscle groups before smaller muscle groups,
    c. perform multijoint exercises at the beginning of a program, and
    d. utilize core exercises before secondary exercises.

- For flexibility, endurance, and balance
  a. use isometric training programs, ROM exercises, flexibility work, and light isotonic training programs;
  b. train smaller muscle groups before larger muscle groups;
  c. perform single-joint exercises at the beginning of a program; and
  d. utilize secondary exercises before core exercises.

It probably is obvious to you by now that we prefer a functional combination that mixes and matches both orders. Having made that declaration, let's discuss some cutting-edge training techniques.

Seven Principles of Training

We can now introduce seven principles and techniques to use and combine in your daily training routine: (1) periodization, (2) split routine, (3) cycling, (4) heavy-light system, (5) supersets, (6) trisets, and (7) pyramiding.

1. Periodization

Many athletes use the periodization principle for training, and this principle is almost always an integral part of any advanced training program. Periodization can be defined as the cycling of loads, volumes, intensity, and exercises in a given time period. The time frame may be divided into days, weeks, months, or even years. Each time frame has its specific arrangement of loads, volumes, intensities, and exercises. Further, the changes in load, volume, and intensity in each cycle of a periodization setup help people avoid overtraining while still making optimal gains in muscular strength, endurance, and power.

The cycles within a periodization can be further broken down into a macrocycle and mesocycle. The *macrocycle* can be termed the same as the complete periodization training time, usually one year. The *mesocycle*, a specific part of the macrocycle training, is usually planned around certain future competitions or events. For example, if you want to compete in a power-lifting contest and one of your lifts is the bench press, you would cycle bench press training in both a macrocycle and mesocycle around this event. The mesocycle itself can be broken down into phases according to the general setup plan of your periodization.

These are the concurrent subdivisions of a mesocycle:

Phase 1. Hypertrophy and endurance training—a training cycle to train the body for gains in muscular endurance or hypertrophy

Phase 2. Strength training—a portion of the program focusing on strength gains (an increase occurs in intensity but overall volume actually decreases)

Phase 3. Power and sport-specific movements—the phase in which sport-specific movements are refined or when an individual focuses on and refines training for a specific season or event (for example, a competitive bodybuilding show)

Phase 4. Competition and maintenance—a phase in the overall program when intensities are lowered and volumes are decreased so the individual can focus on the sport they are competing in or give the body some active rest before beginning another cycle

The example of a training program for a college football player (see table 11.1) gives you an idea of how to set up a periodization schedule. This scheme allows the athlete to focus on specific areas of training (such as muscle hypertrophy) during a specific time period. The focused training allows the body to peak at the correct time for a particular sport event or tournament. And periodization also helps an athlete avoid overtraining.

Table 11.1

SAMPLE PERIODIZATION PROGRAM FOR A COLLEGE FOOTBALL PLAYER

Phase	Dates	Focus	Style
1	January 31-March 15	Hypertrophy	High volume, low intensity
2	March 15-May 22	Strength	Moderate volume, moderate intensity
3	May 22-August 1	Power, sport-specific	Low volume, high intensity
4	August 1-January 31	Competition, maintenance	Low volume, low intensity

Similarly, periodization is a good idea for fitness enthusiasts in general. It allows you to focus training on particular goals during each segment. And it prevents your becoming mentally burned out in any particular program. Plus it helps prevent overtraining.

So there are many benefits of using a periodization setup in your programs. For starters, you can focus your training in and around a certain event or sport. A periodization setup also places planned recovery times in your program. Consistent training at maximum intensities and loads will diminish your gains and decrease your performance. Periodization, however, allows the body to gradually adapt to new stresses placed upon it. It also allows an athlete to peak at the correct time for an event or season.

2. Split Routine

The split system is based on a principle made popular by Boyd Epley for athletes at the University of Nebraska. This program divides up the muscles of the body for training on different days. The advantages to such a routine are that it allows for shorter workouts, for certain muscles to recover and grow while other muscles are working, and for the individual to compete in other activities while weight training without becoming fatigued. The split system also allows you to implement other training principles with it, such as core-secondary exercises and multijoint or single-joint exercises. An example of a split system for the upper body might look like this:

SPLIT-SYSTEM ROUTINE

Monday: chest, shoulders, triceps
Tuesday: back, biceps, lower back, abs
Wednesday: OFF
Thursday: chest, shoulders, triceps
Friday: back, biceps, lower back, abs
Saturday: OFF
Sunday: OFF

3. Cycling

Another advanced training technique, used at the University of Nebraska and at many other collegiate (and professional) institutions, is referred to as the cycling principle. This principle prevents overtraining, and it progressively pushes the body to greater strength gains. The idea behind the principle is that from set to set in an exercise, workout to workout, you change the intensity and volume. This allows the body not to stagnate and fall into a detraining state. The cycling principle fits well into the idea of periodization. Let's look (in table 11.2) at how a core exercise such as the bench press would be used with the cycling principle and fit into a periodization schedule.

Comparing the principle of periodization with the theory of cycling, you can see the fit between these two concepts. Basically, using a cycling principle within a periodization program elicits greater gains in muscular endurance, hypertrophy, strength, and power. It also prevents either your overtraining or your getting into a state of detraining.

4. Heavy-Light System

Still another principle that Boyd Epley proposes is called the heavy-light system. It fits well with the split system and cycling. According to Epley's theory, an individual should train each body part heavily once a week. Then the second time that body part is trained within the same week, it would undergo a light workout. He finds that this guideline elicits the greatest gains for the body in strength, endurance, and power, and it also limits the possibility of overtraining the muscles. The heavy-light system prescribes your heavy workouts being the first workout in the week and your light workouts being the second workout in the week. Table 11.3 gives you an example using the heavy-light system in Phase 2 of a periodization schedule.

You can see in it a change in both the volume (number of sets) of work done and the intensities in the second workouts on Thursday and Friday. This allows for maximum gains in the phase—and more importantly lessens the possibility of injury and overtraining.

5. Supersets

Using a superset, or "super setting," is alternating between two exercises with little or no rest between each set. The superset might

Table 11.2

CYCLING PRINCIPLE FOR
A BENCH PRESS PERIODIZATION SCHEDULE

Phase 1: Hypertrophy or endurance

	Reps	Intensity
Set 1	12	60%
Set 2	12	65%
Set 3	12	70%

Phase 2: Strength

	Reps	Intensity
Set 1	6	75%
Set 2	6	80%
Set 3	6	85%

Phase 3: Power or sport-specific

	Reps	Intensity
Set 1	3	85%
Set 2	3	87%
Set 3	3	90%

Phase 4: Competition or maintenance

	Reps	Intensity
Set 1	10	65%
Set 2	10	70%
Set 3	10	70%

Table 11.3

HEAVY-LIGHT SYSTEM
IN THE PERIODIZATION SCHEDULE S PHASE 2

Phase 2: Strength phase

Monday (heavy): chest, shoulders, triceps
Tuesday (heavy): back, biceps, lower back, abs

Sets	Reps	Intensity
1	8	70%
2	8	72%
3	8	75%

Thursday (light): chest, shoulders, triceps
Friday (light): back, biceps, lower back, abs

Sets	Reps	Intensity
1	8	70%
2	8	70%

involve two exercises for the same body part or entail two exercises for opposing agonist and antagonist muscles. The theory is that the superset principle reduces the time between sets, adds intensity, and places greater loads on the body, resulting in positive advancements in training. Two examples (see table 11.4) will help you gain perspective on the superset.

Be sure you recognize that you are placing greater loads on the body with this technique. You must adjust your recovery time accordingly!

6. Trisets

Advanced training programs also use the triple-set or "triset" principle. A triset is performing (or alternating) three particular exercises in a row before repeating the circuit. Like a superset, the triset principle can be used for a single body part or for three separate body parts. The same theory as for supersets also underlies trisets: increase

Table 11.4

SUPERSET EXERCISES

Superset of two exercises for the same body part

Exercise	Parameters
(1) Biceps barbell curls	3 sets × 10 reps
(2) Seated biceps dumbbell curls	No rest between exercises

Superset of two exercises for an agonist and antagonist

Exercise	Parameters
(2) Biceps cable curls	3 sets × 10 reps
(2) Triceps cable extensions	No rest between exercises

the intensity of the resistance program by increasing the loads and volume and at the same time decreasing the recovery time between exercises. And we again give two examples in table 11.5 of how you might introduce trisets into your training program.

7. Pyramiding

A final advanced training principle we will discuss is pyramiding, which is similar to the cycling principle but goes a step further. Pyramiding involves multiple sets for a single exercise in which you increase the weight used in each set for a predetermined number of sets. Once the increase in weight per set has occurred, you then decrease the weight used in each set for a predetermined amount of sets. The idea is to increase the total volume you are lifting within a specific training session. Table 11.6 gives an example of how a pyramiding scheme would be introduced for a bench press.

All seven of these principles can be integrated into advanced training programs. Understand, however, that increases in your loads, intensity, and volumes require that you also adjust recovery time accordingly to prevent overtraining or injury.

Table 11.5

TRISET EXERCISES

Triset of three exercises for the same body part

Exercise	Parameters
(1) Biceps barbell curls	3 sets × 10 reps
(2) Seated biceps dumbbell curls	No rest between exercises
(3) Hammer curls	

Triset of three exercises for three different body parts

Exercise	Parameters
(1) Wide-grip chins	3 sets × 10 reps
(2) Flat bench flys	No rest between exercises
(3) Seated dumbbell shoulder press	

Table 11.6

PYRAMID

Set	Reps	Load (lbs.)
1	12	165
2	10	190
3	8	220
4	10	185
5	12	155

CHAPTER 12

Designing Training Programs

Before designing any training program, you must determine the goals and appropriate parameters of your personal training constraints or needs. This chapter begins by guiding you through that process. Then it develops a series of upper-body training programs for beginners through advanced lifters. A section focusing on a sport-specific program is also included. Veterans of the fitness lifestyle can pick and choose exercises for a program that they feel will be useful to them. In short, from the material in this chapter you can select the components for your personal program and design it to meet your specific training needs.

Designing a Personal Program

Each resistance-training program has different goals, exercises, and variables. The first step for training is to determine personal needs. The second step is to find a training program to meet those needs. This requires a "needs analysis" and the development of training goals. Unless you first spend a little time on this analysis and goal setting, your efforts are not working as efficiently as possible, which in turn lessens your results.

Needs Analysis and Training Goals

A needs analysis essentially entails determining what requirements your training program must meet. Assess carefully what areas need improvement. For example, if you're a swimmer and notice that a high level of fatigue develops in your upper arms when you're competing, you might determine that your training program should be geared toward improving the local muscular endurance of the upper-arm region. Your analysis process aims at first noting what areas need attention in your training program. If you're a body-builder, on the other hand, you might notice a visible need for improvement in the size of the chest area. These are simple examples of needs analysis.

The next step is mapping out your training goals, using the information from your needs analysis. Choosing from this list of goals for weight training, for instance, you can focus on areas that need improvement. You might decide on a single goal or develop a combination of all these areas:

Weight-Training Goals
1. Improved flexibility
2. Increased muscular endurance
3. Muscle hypertrophy
4. Improved power
5. Muscle balance

As you can see, your training program can be fine-tuned to meet your needs and goals. Most training programs follow a sequence.

Order of Resistance-Training Program

An ideal resistance-training program follows this sequence, which ensures optimal ratios of flexibility, joint stabilization, injury prevention, and resistance exercise.

1. General Warm-Up

The general warm-up includes a modality that raises your core body temperature a few degrees and allows your muscular system to prepare itself for the stresses that will be placed on it throughout your program. The main concern at this point is to warm up the body, work some range-of-motion exercise into the system, and ready the body for greater amounts of exercise. A warm-up can consist of a jog, pedaling on the stationary bike, or other activity that achieves this goal of warm-up.

2. Flexibility Exercises

After completing a general warm-up, you move into the series of flexibility exercises given in chapter 3. Remember that flexibility work should be performed *prior* to any resistance-training exercises. The goal of these exercises is to provide a "wake-up call" to all the tissues in the muscular system. A second goal is to work the joints and muscles through their complete ranges of motion in the three movement planes of the body.

3. Joint-Stabilization Exercises

Next you move to joint-stabilization exercises (see chapter 4). These exercises provide a muscular balance, using elastic cords, bodywork, and light dumbbells. This muscular balance is between the small muscles and tissues surrounding skeletal joints and the large primary movers of the muscular system. Remember, a lack of balance between these large and small tissues can result in injury and a decline in performance. After completing these three categories, you are ready to move on to the resistance-training exercises in your program.

4. Resistance Exercises

You now start on the core resistance exercises. The series of exercises you add will depend on your goals and previous training experience. In other words, design your resistance-training programs in terms of your goals and experience. It's worth reviewing here what you must know to properly organize your program.

The resistance exercises you implement into the program should revolve around the principles of core and secondary exercises. Core exercises are resistance exercises that recruit all the muscles in specific groups as you train. For example, the dumbbell shoulder press utilizes a concentric and eccentric action of the entire musculature group constituting the shoulder. A secondary exercise focuses on a specific muscle or part of a muscle group. The side lateral raise is a secondary exercise: it focuses on one area, the lateral head of the deltoid, and tends to recruit fewer fibers from the surrounding areas of the deltoid.

In effect, we have now broadened the proper training sequence to five items: (1) warm-up, (2) flexibility exercises, (3) joint-stabilization exercises, (4) core strength-training exercises, and (5) secondary strength-training exercises. And these specific strength-training exercises depend on your goals and level, or the parameters of your training program, as determined by a needs analysis. We will now develop some sample conditioning programs, for beginner to advanced-level workouts.

Level 1—Starting and General Health Conditioning

Many people find great use in having a general conditioning program. It is an ideal program to start with as an introduction to resistance training. Furthermore, general conditioning is a good choice for individuals looking to receive enhanced fitness without any specific goals in mind other than improving their health. The guidelines for the program are listed in the next section. The program combines all facets of information in this book, and it will definitely improve your overall fitness levels.

If you are a beginner and looking to move forward in your resistance training, expect to spend the first 8 to 12 weeks with this format. After that time you can move forward.

Guidelines for Beginner and General Fitness Conditioning

A general conditioning program is useful for the beginner who is new to resistance training. And it is also an excellent program to use for general fitness purposes. It allows you to maintain a healthy lifestyle, prevent injury, and improve overall conditioning.

As a beginner, looking toward advancing your resistance training in the future, follow this program *for a minimum of six to eight weeks.* This time frame will allow your body to adapt to resistance and prepare itself for a more advanced program. Remember to follow the correct program sequence, which begins with a general warm-up and moves through your core exercises. You will begin to notice changes in body composition over time. Most beginners first notice that the weights are more "comfortable" to use, as a result of the neuromuscular system's becoming familiar with the new movements that have been introduced into the body's system. This result usually occurs over the first four weeks. At the same time, changes in body composition will begin to occur and increase as you progress and become more advanced.

Program for Beginner and General Fitness Conditioning

We give a typical upper body program here, selecting exercises from the previous chapters. This program is for beginners who are new to resistance training, people returning to training after an absence from it, and those interested in general conditioning for overall health.

Frequency:
3 times per week

Training Principles
1. Injury prevention
2. Overall conditioning
3. Light resistance

Program Components in Order
1. Warm-up
2. Flexibility work
3. Joint-stabilization work
4. Upper-body circuit training in these ways:
   - One exercise per body part
   - Doing 10 to 15 repetitions per exercise
   - Completing a single set per exercise
5. Core Exercises:
   - Barbell bench press
   - Wide-grip lat pull-down
   - Seated shoulder press
   - Biceps barbell curl
   - Triceps cable push-downs

Level 2–Intermediate Training

The intermediate training program is the next step to follow if you are advancing through our series of resistance-training programs. This is the second step for either the fitness enthusiast or aspiring body-builder with no prior experience in resistance training.

If you are an athlete without any prior experience in resistance training, too, this is an ideal "stepping-stone" program for more advanced routines. One recommendation for the athlete would be to implement some sport-specific exercise at the beginning of this program. These exercises should be relevant to the sport in which you participate. We will discuss some sport-specific programs later in this chapter.

The bodybuilder or fitness enthusiast should progress through the intermediate program and on to the advanced program when ready. Remember, the only difference between bodybuilding and general fitness training is the volume, loads, and intensity in which the weights are lifted. The fitness enthusiast and bodybuilder will, in general, train by using the same exercises and similar programs.

If you have successfully completed the general conditioning program for a period of six to eight weeks, or are an individual who has had a minimal experience (training level) of about three months, the intermediate program is where you want to begin. The goal of the intermediate program is to implement more advanced training principles to achieve more specific goals.

At this point your body has probably adapted to resistance training, so it's time to focus your program on the overload principle. The intermediate program should be used for a period of *three to six months*. During this time you should begin to implement more and more principles of resistance training. Let's begin by laying out the guidelines and lining up the training principles you will eventually implement.

Guidelines for Intermediate Training

First, at this point in your training it is time to become goal specific. Determine what the overall goals for your training are, and begin to work toward them. Decide if you want to train your body for endurance, strength or size, power or balance. Once you've decided on the focus of your program, you can select the training variables. The only real difference among general, intermediate, and advanced training programs is intensity and frequency.

The following sample intermediate program is laid out for an individual looking to increase strength and size. You would use different repetition levels for programs geared toward muscle endurance, strength, and power, setting up a program according to your desired outcome.

Bodybuilders predominantly train in a repetition base or range of 8 to 12 reps per set. This repetition level coincides with maximum gains in muscle size and is conducive to hypertrophy. A fitness enthusiast, however, would gear training toward a wider spectrum of repetitions, looking to increase a combination of strength, power, and endurance of the muscle. A fitness enthusiast would probably train in a repetition spectrum ranging from 5 to 15 repetitions per set. Consider an example of how this wide variety of training repetitions could be met: you might train completely for muscular endurance (15 reps or higher) for one workout, and then switch to a muscular, strength-focused workout (6 to 12 repetitions per set) for the next workout.

Another setup could work as well: you would train for muscular endurance for two to four weeks, and then switch to a muscular strength program for four weeks. Athletes, on the other hand, should analyze or determine what the sport "asks" of the body. Does the sport (such as swimming) require large amounts of muscular endurance, or does it (in the case of football) require muscular power? Once you have determined what the requirements of the sport are, you can devise a proper repetition spectrum.

Before you jump into the intermediate program, take a minute for review; that way, the "walk-through" of the program will be quite easy. The program listed next is an intermediate program designed to develop muscular size and strength. It is *not* geared toward a specific sport or athletic endeavor. This following program creates a base training guide for an individual with a limited amount of exposure to resistance training. It is set up to flexibly allow you to add exercises, repetitions, or sets according to your own personal goals.

More advanced training principles are added to the intermediate program. You might find it useful to review chapter 11 for information on split-system training, cycling, multiple sets, and repetition variation.

Intermediate Program for Strength and Size

Frequency:
3 times per week

Training Principles
1. Split system
2. Cycling

3. Multiple sets
4. Repetition variation

Program Components in Order

1. Warm-up
2. Flexibility work
3. Joint-stabilization work
4. Upper-body resistance training in these ways:
   - Doing three sets per exercise
   - Split system
   - Cycling
   - Heavy-light days

INTERMEDIATE-LEVEL PROGRAM (STRENGTH AND SIZE)

MONDAY

WEEK 1

Exercise	Sets	Reps	Intensity levels (% of 1RM)
1. Barbell bench presses	3	10	65, 70, 75
2. Incline dumbbell presses	3	10	65, 70, 75
3. Flat bench dumbbell flys	3	10	65, 70, 75
4. Wide-grip lat pull-downs	3	10	65, 70, 75
5. T-bar rows	3	10	65, 70, 75

WEDNESDAY

Exercise	Sets	Reps	Intensity levels (% of 1RM)
1. Barbell shoulder presses	3	10	65, 70, 75
2. Barbell upright rows	3	10	65, 70, 75
3. Biceps barbell curls	3	10	65, 70, 75
4. Triceps French presses	3	10	65, 70, 75

FRIDAY

Exercise	Sets	Reps	Intensity levels (% of 1RM)
1. Barbell bench presses	2	10	65, 70
2. Incline dumbbell presses	2	10	65, 70
3. Flat bench dumbbells	2	10	65, 70
4. Wide-grip lat pull-downs	2	10	65, 70
5. Close-grip cable rows	2	10	65, 70
6. T-bar rows	2	10	65, 70

INTERMEDIATE-LEVEL PROGRAM (STRENGTH AND SIZE)

WEEK 2

MONDAY

Exercise	Sets	Reps	Intensity levels (% of 1RM)
1. Barbell shoulder presses	2	10	65, 70
2. Barbell upright rows	2	10	65, 70
3. Biceps barbell curls	2	10	65, 70
4. Triceps French presses	2	10	65, 70

WEDNESDAY

Exercise	Sets	Reps	Intensity levels (% of 1RM)
1. Barbell bench presses	3	8	70, 75, 80
2. Incline dumbbell presses	3	8	70, 75, 80
3. Flat bench dumbbells	3	8	70, 75, 80
4. Wide-grip lat pull-downs	3	8	70, 75, 80
5. Close-grip cable rows	3	8	70, 75, 80
6. T-bar rows	3	8	70, 75, 80

FRIDAY

Exercise	Sets	Reps	Intensity levels (% of 1RM)
1. Barbell shoulder presses	3	10	70, 75, 80
2. Barbell upright rows	3	10	70, 75, 80
3. Biceps barbell curls	3	10	70, 75, 80
4. Triceps French presses	3	10	70, 75, 80

This outline gives you a sample of an intermediate muscular strength program. It entails the complete upper body workouts for a period of two weeks. After two weeks you could repeat the same program or change it. You would decide individually what exercises, sets per exercise, and repetitions are working. If there are areas you feel are not moving in accordance to your goals, implement the changes that need to be made.

Each person is individual, an important point to remember, and every training program needs to be tailored to meet the specific needs of the individual. There is no "cookie cutter" program that can result in each individual's achieving his or her goals. You can find exercises and programs laid out that are specific to meeting certain goals and training muscular systems in a specified way. Even with these programs and exercises, you must alter features to meet the requirements of each individual.

A baseball player, for example, who has sound structure nevertheless begins to develop fatigue in the backside of the shoulder (the scapular region). The baseball player has been on a program specifically designed to prepare the body for the stresses placed on it by playing, but for some reason his shoulder is fatiguing. Therefore, some modifications *must* be made to his training program to individualize it.

With all this in mind, you have a proper perspective to use the outline or basic setup of the intermediate program. As with all the information in this book, you should individualize it to your goals.

Level 3—Advanced Training

The advanced training program you develop can be similar to your intermediate program. You use the split-system, heavy-light system, cycling, and periodization principles. The principal difference is that the volumes, loads, and intensity become greater. The frequency of training also increases, coupled with the predetermined periodization scheme you develop. And, like the intermediate program, the advanced program outline is only a base from which to individualize to meet your specific needs.

Guidelines for Advanced Training

Only individuals with at least six months of training experience should use the advanced program. Before beginning this phase of training, be completely comfortable with the principles introduced in the intermediate phase. Even so, it is a good idea to review the principles before mapping out your program, so you are sure to use them to greatest benefit.

Remember, as with the intermediate program, be goal specific. Set up your program to specifically meet your goals. For example, a bodybuilder will train for muscular size. The loads, volumes, and intensity of the training program will be geared toward the goal of an increase in muscular size. A swimmer, on the other hand, has a goal in mind of improving performance for a competition. She will select exercises, repetitions, and set variances to optimize physical performance in the pool. Use all the principles described in previous chapters to tailor this advanced program to meet the needs of the goals you have set up. Take the time to begin with a needs analysis, set your goals, and develop a training program that allows you to meet these goals.

At this level you should begin to plan out your training schedule in a periodization format that includes different phases. The phases may be set up to synchronize with a competitive event you are training for or in accordance with some other goal.

Begin to plan your training in a year-round or six-month periodization. Look to set up different phases with distinct goals to achieve at the end of each planned phase. Say you are a recreational volleyball player, for instance, and have numerous tournaments in the summer months. In that case, the periodization schedule and training would be focused toward your competitive season, which occurs three months out of the year.

Your training at the advanced level needs to be specific. Train specific to what your goals are: muscle endurance, size or strength, or power. Develop your program around one of these areas, and adjust your loads, volumes, intensity, and frequency accordingly. The overall primary goal of a power lifter, for example, is an increase in muscular strength. The individual's workouts are geared toward muscular strength, and the periodization schedule focuses toward participation in particular competitions within a year's time frame. A bodybuilder would set up a similar periodization schedule, one delineated against the calendar of bodybuilding contests to participate in over the year, and one with the overall goal of the individual workouts enhancing the bodybuilder's muscular size.

You can see from these examples that once a certain level of training has been reached, the goals of each workout and the entire training program become very specific. That is why it so important to set up your goals and develop your training program accordingly. Next, we give the guidelines for an advanced training program. Always remember to individualize them specifically to your training programs.

Program for Advanced Training

The advanced program introduces supersets, trisets, and pyramiding into the training scheme. Adhere to all the principles of periodization, cycling, the split system, and the heavy-light system to receive the greatest benefits from your program.

The advanced program follows the same order in setup as all other programs we have recommended in this book: (1) warm-up, (2) flexibility exercises, (3) joint-stabilization exercises, (4) core exercises, (5) secondary exercises. Following this sequence produces a proper warm-up, helps prevent injury, and is goal specific in format.

The overall goal of this particular sample advanced program is the development of muscular size. It includes the use of multiple sets, in which different percentages of your 1RM are used. For example, on Monday (which is a heavy day), for the second set of the bench press you would use 75 percent of your 1RM. Remember that this program is only a base to use for individualizing to your own specific goals.

In this advanced training program, geared toward increases in muscle strength, the only additional principles introduced are the systematic usage of supersets (two exercises for the same body part), pyramids (increasing the weight each set for a specific exercise), and trisets (three exercises for the same body part).

Frequency:
4 times per week

Training Principles
1. Split system
2. Cycling
3. Multiple sets
4. Repetition variation
5. Pyramiding
6. Supersets
7. Trisets

Program Components in Order

1. Warm-up
2. Flexibility work
3. Joint-stabilization work
4. Upper-body resistance training
   - Three to four sets per exercise
   - Split system
   - Cycling
   - Heavy-light system
   - Pyramids
   - Supersets
   - Trisets

ADVANCED-LEVEL PROGRAM (STRENGTH AND SIZE)

WEEK 1 (HEAVY DAYS)

MONDAY

Exercise	Sets	Reps	Intensity levels (% of 1RM)
1. Barbell bench presses	4	10, 8, 6, 10	65, 75, 80, 65
2. Incline dumbbell presses	3	10	65, 70, 75
3. Supersets of flat bench dumbbell flys and decline dumbbell flys	3	10	65
4. Wide-grip lat pull-downs	4	10, 8, 6, 10	65, 75, 80, 65
5. Close-grip cable rows	3	10	65, 70, 75
6. Supersets of T-bar rows and close-grip cable pull-downs	3	10	65

TUESDAY

Exercise	Sets	Reps	Intensity levels (% of 1RM)
1. Barbell shoulder presses	4	10, 8, 6, 10	65, 75, 80, 65
2. Trisets of barbell upright rows, dumbbell side-lateral raises, and rear-lateral dumbbell raises*	3	10	65
3. Supersets of biceps barbell curls and biceps dumbbell curls	4	10	65
4. Supersets of triceps French and triceps cable press-downs	3	10	65

*Repeat each exercise in order at 65% of 1RM for each series of three sets.

ADVANCED-LEVEL PROGRAM (STRENGTH AND SIZE)

WEEK 1 (LIGHT DAYS)

THURSDAY

Exercise	Sets	Reps	Intensity levels (% of 1RM)
1. Barbell bench presses	3	10	65, 70, 65
2. Incline dumbbell presses	3	10	65, 70, 65
3. Flat bench dumbbell flys	3	10	65, 70, 65
4. Wide-grip lat pull-downs	3	10	65, 70, 65
5. Close-grip cable rows	3	10	65, 70, 65
6. T-bar rows	3	10	65, 70, 65

FRIDAY

Exercise	Sets	Reps	Intensity levels (% of 1RM)
1. Barbell shoulder presses	3	10	65, 70, 65
2. Barbell upright rows	2	10	65, 70
3. Side-lateral dumbbell raises	2	10	65, 70
4. Biceps barbell curls	3	10	65, 70, 65
5. Biceps cable curls	2	10	65, 70
6. Triceps French presses	3	10	65, 70, 65
7. Triceps cable press-downs	2	10	65, 70

ADVANCED-LEVEL PROGRAM (STRENGTH AND SIZE)

WEEK 2 (HEAVY DAYS)

MONDAY

Exercise	Sets	Reps	Intensity levels (% of 1RM)
1. Barbell bench presses	4	10, 8, 6, 6, 10	65, 75, 80, 85, 65
2. Incline dumbbell presses	4	10	65, 70, 75, 65
3. Supersets of flat bench dumbbell presses and decline dumbbell presses	2	10	65
4. Wide-grip lat pull-downs	4	10, 8, 6, 6, 10	65, 75, 80, 85, 65
5. Close-grip cable rows	4	10	65, 70, 75, 65
6. Supersets of T-bar rows and close-grip cable pull-downs	2	10	65

TUESDAY

Exercise	Sets	Reps	Intensity levels (% of 1RM)
1. Barbell shoulder presses	4	10, 8, 6, 10	65, 75, 80, 65
2. Trisets of barbell upright rows, dumbbell side-lateral raises, and rear-lateral dumbbell raises	4	10	65
3. Supersets of biceps barbell curls and biceps dumbbell curls	3	10	65
4. Supersets of triceps French presses and triceps cable press-downs	3	10	65

ADVANCED-LEVEL PROGRAM (STRENGTH AND SIZE)

WEEK 2 (LIGHT DAYS)

THURSDAY

Exercise	Sets	Reps	Intensity levels (% of 1RM)
1. Barbell bench presses	2	10	65, 70
2. Incline dumbbell presses	2	10	65, 70
3. Flat bench dumbbell flys	2	10	65, 70
4. Wide-grip lat pull-downs	2	10	65, 70
5. Close-grip cable rows	2	10	65, 70
6. T-bar rows	2	10	65, 70

FRIDAY

Exercise	Sets	Reps	Intensity levels (% of 1RM)
1. Barbell shoulder presses	2	10	65, 70
2. Barbell upright rows	2	10	65, 70
3. Side-lateral dumbbell raises	2	10	65, 70
4. Biceps barbell curls	2	10	65, 70
5. Biceps cable curls	2	10	65, 70
6. Triceps French presses	2	10	65, 70
7. Triceps cable press-downs	2	10	65, 70

Sport-Specific Training Program

Sport-specific training is an advanced program that uses all the training principles we have been discussing—geared specifically to the needs of a particular sport. Sport-specific training has one basic principle: plan your training program around the specific requirements of your sport. In general, you want to first analyze or break down the movements, energy requirements, and other parameters of your sport and then match your training program to these.

Guidelines for Setting Up Sport-Specific Training

To set up a sport-specific program, first do a needs analysis of the sport. What physical requirements does the sport make? What areas of the body are frequently injured in the sport? Is the sport based more on muscular power or endurance? List questions that pertain to the physical needs of the sport along with your answers.

Next look at the movement patterns of the sport. Once you have reviewed the biomechanics of the sport, you can develop a list of specific resistance-training exercises that can strengthen the body according to the sport's demands. Then you're ready to lay out a program.

Use a periodization scheme that works around your competitive season or peaks your body for specific events. But also remember that the goals of a sport-specific program are both to prevent injury and optimize performance levels.

Consider an example of thinking about these twin goals of injury prevention and improved performance for the sport of golf. If you are an avid or competitive golfer, don't train with heavy weights or push to muscle failure right before your match. Golf is a "touch" sport. Prime mover work and muscle failure impede the interaction of nerves and synergists and adversely affect the feel of swinging the club and the ball strike, especially when you're putting. Give yourself a 48-hour window of recovery time after the heavy work; instead train for flexibility, joint stabilization, or endurance during the two days prior to competition.

Let's now look at how a sport-specific program might be laid out. We will also provide some sample programs for collegiate and professional athletes.

Sport-Specific Program

Frequency:
4 to 6 times per week

Training Principles

1. Split system
2. Cycling
3. Multiple sets
4. Repetition variation
5. Pyramiding

Program Components in Order

1. Warm-up
2. Flexibility work
3. Joint-stabilization work
4. Sport-specific resistance exercises

Most athletics are "total body" in action. When we speak of total body, we refer to the idea that the entire body is used in athletic competition. Your body is set in a specific anatomical position, and biomechanical actions occur in integrated movement patterns. For example, when a baseball player is swinging the bat, he places the body in a certain batting stance; he strides with the feet, rotates the hips, extends with the arms to swing the bat (through a specified integrated movement pattern) and hits the baseball. As you might guess, specific exercises and training guidelines need to be implemented for each phase of the swing. This all can be summed up by saying that your entire body and all its muscles—from feet to fingertips—are used in athletic competition.

For this reason we provide you with only a skeleton outline from which to develop a sound sport-specific program. All the information about training the arms and upper body, as important as it is to the development of a sport-specific program, is still only a part of training, work to be expanded to encompass the entire body.

In Conclusion

Competitive athletes in the 1960s and 1970s never got beat; they got "out-milligrammed." They rehabbed; they didn't prehab. They

PROGRAM GUIDELINES FOR THREE REALMS OF ACTIVITIES

	Activity	Training goal
1. Throwing and striking sports	Golf Tennis Racquetball Softball Volleyball	Flexibility work Muscle endurance work Muscle balance work
2. General fitness	Walking and jogging Water activities	Flexibility work Stamina work Muscle balance work
3. Bodybuilding	Shaping Muscle building	Muscle hypertrophy work Muscle power work

guessed at what they didn't know. This generation worked before video, before motion analysis, before computers, before the Internet, and, believe it or not, even before Nintendo! Sport science didn't exist, and sports medicine was still in its infancy.

As part of the ACL-meniscus learning curve of that era, I (Tom House) had seven knee surgeries and reconstructions, with immobilizing casts and giant scars that today would require nothing more than a simple arthroscope and three weeks of physical therapy. Conditioning coaches weren't even a consideration. In fact, coaches told athletes in the 1960s and 1970s not to lift weights. There was no Gatorade and no 40-40-20-diet plan. Players took salt pills, drank beer after workouts to replenish body fluids, and chewed tobacco to fight cottonmouth. Pregame they ate steak and eggs, French fried potatoes, almost anything. Postgame, well, if you could still read the menu, it wasn't time to eat!

So, you say, who cares? Why look into the past? Here's the point. You now live in the information age, and your potential knowledge base is growing exponentially. Through the schooling of trial and error, the "middle-aged" generation knows a lot of what *doesn't* work. Combine the two eras and change your paradigm. Apply any, or all, of what this book has taught you to your daily work and play.

Identify your priorities, set some goals, determine some achievable objectives, help your body find form and function. Remember the mental-emotional mantra, "Every long journey is begun by one small step." Start your fitness journey with stronger arms and upper body as a first step.

ABOUT THE AUTHORS

Sean M. Cochran, a strength and conditioning consultant in the San Diego area, has consulted with many collegiate athletic organizations, such as the University of San Diego and the University of California—San Diego. He also has consulted many professional baseball clubs and professional athletes from a wide variety of sports.

Completing a masters degree in sports medicine, Cochran is a member of the American College of Sports Medicine and is certified by the National Strength and Conditioning Association and the Chiropractic Rehabilitation Association. He is the conditioning coordinator for Functional Fitness Paradigms, which develops conditioning programs for the public and athletes. He is also a member of the USA Weightlifting Federation and coaches on the club level. He has been involved in three fitness videos, and his manual, *Torso Medicine Ball Training*, details extension, flexion, and rotational exercises for the lower back and abdominal muscles. Cochran lives in San Diego, California.

Tom House is one of the world's foremost authorities on upper body strength and conditioning. His company, Bio-Kinetics, helps athletes maximize their performance through proper biomechanics in such sports as baseball, softball, tennis, golf, and volleyball. A Major League Baseball pitcher from 1967 to 1979 for Atlanta, Boston, and Seattle, House went on to coach pitchers for the Houston Astros, San Diego Padres, and Texas Rangers—including Hall of Famer Nolan Ryan. He also has coached in Japan and Latin America. House has authored eight books on baseball and eight instructional videos on pitching, including *Fit to Pitch* (Human Kinetics, 1996) and the second edition of *The Pitching Edge* (Human Kinetics, 1999). In 1998 he was presented with the American Baseball Coaches Association's lifetime achievement award. House lives in Del Mar, California.

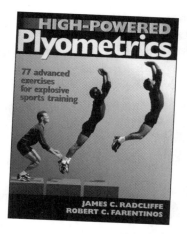